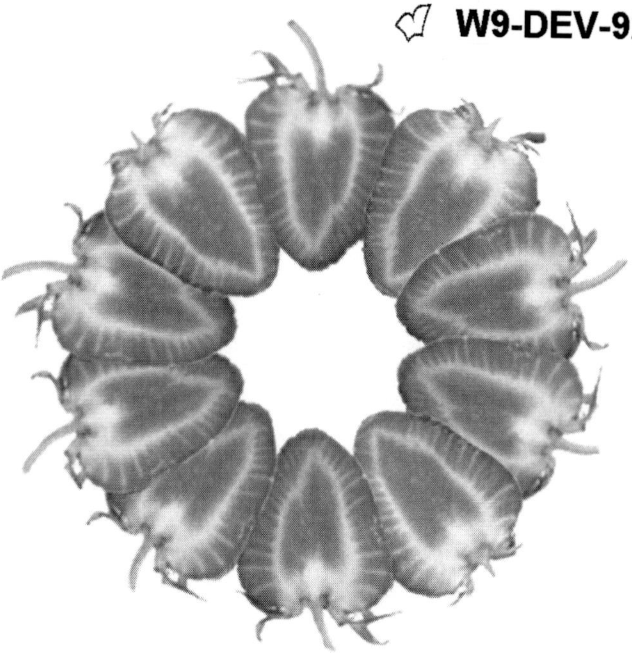

THE TEN LOVES OF GOD

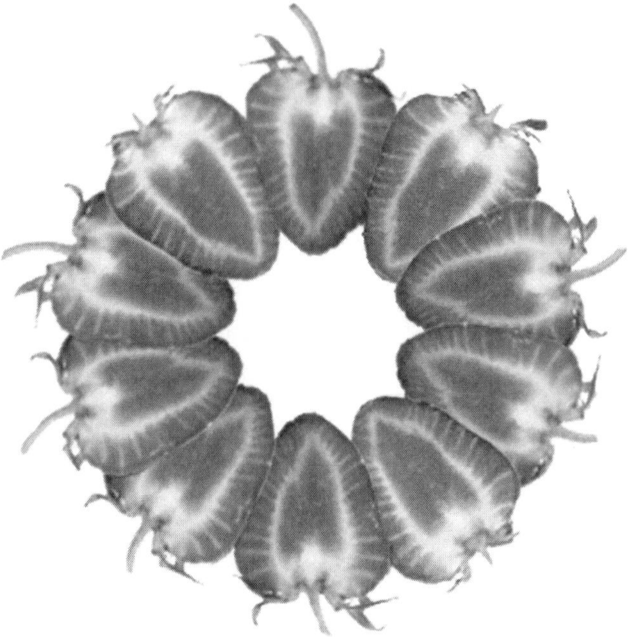

THE TEN LOVES OF GOD

A devotional and small group study on God's Ten Commandments

DR. WIN GREEN

TATE PUBLISHING *& Enterprises*

Bible Translations Used: LB, GN, TEV, RSV, KJV, NRSV, Good News, Phillips, The Message

Published by Tate Publishing & Enterprises, LLC
127 E. Trade Center Terrace | Mustang, Oklahoma 73064 USA
1.888.361.9473 | www.tatepublishing.com

Tate Publishing is committed to excellence in the publishing industry. The company reflects the philosophy established by the founders, based on Psalm 68:11,
"The Lord gave the word and great was the company of those who published it."

Cover design by Lauran Levy
Interior design by Joel Uber

Published in the United States of America

ISBN: 978-1-61739-016-6
1. Religion; Biblical Meditations, Old Testament
2. Religion; Christian Life, Spiritual Growth
10.12.16

For my love, Stephanie!
Yo te amo con todo mi corazon!

Acknowledgments

My home is alive with the sounds that young families make—full of crashes, shrieks, and laughter. I write in the middle of this maelstrom. I succeed because of the love, care, and organizational genius of my bride, Stephanie. Besides being my inspiration and best editor, Stephanie also manages our household with grace, aplomb, and efficiency. Scripture makes the ultimate understatement, "He who finds a wife finds a good thing." Amen!

My heartfelt thanks go to the churches who inspired me to think through the Ten Commandments, and who offered great feedback whenever I preached them: Everglades Community Church of Pembroke Pines, Florida, and The Nassau Christian Center of Princeton, New Jersey. Both congregations blessed me and my family. And special thanks go to the office staff of the Nassau Christian Center: George Bilyeu, Ester Davidson, and Robin Siegel who patiently listened as I read them draft after draft. They generously shared their feedback, which made this book much, much better. Thank you!

My gratitude is extended to George Gallup, Maxie Dunnam, and Professor Yolanda Pierce for reading through this book and giving it their endorsement. I am supremely proud to have the name of each on the back of this book!

A special shout-out to Charles Kim who helped me rethink and rewrite portions of this book! Friend and colleague in ministry, Charles provided a special spark to key sections. Thanks!

Several individuals edited different chapters of this book, adding their insights and feedback. They generously shared that which is most precious—their time. Jerry Riest challenged me to elevate my thinking on a number of different issues involving the sixth commandment in particular. Spencer and Kat Silverglate, both stupendous writers, took time out to read through my manuscript and turn my scribbling into something coherent. You both are the best. Brian George, my prayer partner, read through sections of this book and offered his encouragement and support at a critical time. Dick Pershan is the most literate person I know, and he generously condescended to edit this work. Mike Montgomery, the finest patent attorney I know, read through my manuscript with his eye for detail. He is the most patient man I know, and one of the kindest friends I have.

I would also like to thank the Florida Annual Conference of the United Methodist Church, and its bishop—Timothy Whitaker—who supported me . Thank you.

Finally, I want to thank my family: My brothers, Drew and Raleigh, and my sister, Cliffeton, read through portions of this book and offered several excellent insights. My mother-in-law, Rhoda Kingston, read through this manuscript and offered me her unvarnished perspective which kept me going at a critical time. My father-in-law, Alan Kingston, read through the book with his eye for detail and helped spot the errors that no one else would. A huge thank you with love.

Table of Contents

PREFACE:
How to Use This Book

This book has two complementary purposes.

It is first a devotional book, intended to inspire and edify individuals who read it. Each of the ten chapters focuses on one of the Ten Commandments. For personal use, I suggest that you read this book at a pace of one chapter a day. After finishing each chapter, it is best to give yourself time to reflect on what God might be saying to you through what you've read. Again, this book's first purpose is to help you grow spiritually by guiding you through a personal reflection on each of the Ten Commandments, and applying them to your life.

The book's second purpose is to facilitate a small group study and discussion. It is hoped that Sunday school classes, small growth groups, and Bible studies will use this book as a twelve-week study. Every chapter concludes with an outline for group discussion. Ideally, each participant will have read the preceding chapter before their group's weekly meeting. A facilitator will then lead the group through the questions at chapter's end while keeping an eye on the clock. The questions are designed to stimulate discussion. This study does not strive to articulate right and wrong answers. Instead, it is a study intended to help the reader experience the meaning and application of the Ten Commandments.

I hope and pray that this book will bless you!

The Ten Commandments

One:
You shall have no other gods before me

Two:
You shall not make for yourself a carved image—any likeness *of anything* that *is* in heaven above, or that *is* in the earth beneath, or that *is* in the water under the earth; you shall not bow down to them nor serve them. For I, the Lord your God, *am* a jealous God, visiting the iniquity of the fathers upon the children to the third and fourth *generations* of those who hate Me, but showing mercy to thousands, to those who love Me and keep My commandments.

Three:
You shall not take the name of the Lord your God in vain, for the Lord will not hold *him* guiltless who takes His name in vain.

Four:
Remeber the Sabbath day, to keep it holy. Six days you shall labor and do all your work, but the seventh day *is* the Sabbath of the Lord your God. *In it* you shall do no work: you, nor your son, nor your daughter, nor your male servant, nor your female servant,

nor your cattle, nor your stranger who *is* within your gates. For *in* six days the LORD made the heavens and earth, the sea, and all that *is* in them, and rested the seventh day. Therefore the LORD blessed the Sabbath day and hallowed it.

FIVE:
Honor your father and your mother, that your days may be long upon the land which the LORD your God is giving you.

SIX:
You shall not murder.

SEVEN:
You shall not commit adultery.

EIGHT:
You shall not steal.

NINE:
You shall not bear false witness against your neighbor.

TEN:
You shall not covet your neighbor's house; you shall not covet your neighbor's wife, nor his male servant, nor his female servant, nor his ox, nor his donkey, nor anything that *is* your neighbor's.

Command One:
My God Is Bigger Than Your God!

In Woody Allen's film *Crimes and Misdemeanors,* Judah Rosenthal is a successful optometrist enjoying a hot affair with a fetching young flight attendant. All was bliss until his lover surprised him with a threat—that she would tell Judah's wife about their relationship if he did not file for divorce. Judah is counseled by a rabbi to confess everything to his wife, Miriam, but he ignores the advice, fearing the loss of his marriage. Instead, he turns to his brother-in-law who hires a hit man to murder the mistress. Guilt-stricken over the adultery and murder, Judah does a sudden about face and returns to the beliefs of his devout Jewish childhood. For the first time in his adult life, he fears a holy judgment and suffers from visions of an all-seeing God. He lives in anguish. But then the unexpected happens, with the passage of time he is surprised to find that his guilt fades, and with it, his fear of God. By the end of the film, Judah's life returns to "normal"—a life without religion or remorse. The murder is eventually pinned to a drifter with a criminal record, letting Judah off the hook. Woody Allen ends his film pushing his audience to ask the obvious question:

Is there a God?

Incredibly enough, this question, "Is there a God?" is being answered the world over with a resounding "*Yes!*" God is thriving in the modern world like never before! Let me share some compelling illustrations.

- Attachment to the world's four biggest religions–Christianity, Islam, Buddhism, and Hinduism–rose from 67% in 1900 to 73% in 2005 ![1]
- 84% of the Russian people now report believing in God[2] even after three generations of intense communist education against religious faith. Prime Minister Vladimir Putin even has his own private chapel next door to his office in the Kremlin.
- By 2050 China is poised to become the world's largest Muslim AND Christian nation even though the country is still officially atheist!

The doom of organized religion has been prophesized by the cultured scoffers for the past thee hundred years, and yet faith in God is spreading faster than ever before. The very things that were supposed to kill religion: freedom, education, and technology, have in fact turbocharged its spread. Each day in Asia, 50,000 new souls commit themselves to Jesus Christ, and in Africa the growth is 20,000 per day! There are now 2.5 billion Christian believers the world over! But as dynamic as Christian growth is, it is surpassed by Islam. At its current rate, Islam is poised to overtake Christianity as the world's most populous religion by the year 2050!

And such growth is not limited to Christianity and Islam. In China, the Falun Gong religion, established only in 1992, already has millions of followers. Hinduism has an annual growth rate of 1.84 percent and claims 870 million adherents. Buddhism continues to thrive in the East, while making inroads in the West.

Naturally, all this religious growth comes with tension. With a few strokes on a computer keyboard, it is possible to learn how different religions agree and disagree. Attempts are made to harmonize various the differences, but they fail the acid test of logic. After all, the Jews are staunch believers in one God, but the Hindus rejoice in many. The Christians claim a Trinitarian God in three persons, but Muslims insist Allah must be one. Mormons trumpet a God who offers many levels of heaven, but some Buddhists dismiss heaven altogether. But even with such differences, most of the world's people agree on the most basic concern of all—that God exists.

So now comes the hard part—defining who God is. Indeed, this may be the great challenge of the 21st century—defining God. Our politically correct world isn't comfortable defining God because to do so highlights the differences, and people shy away from religious differences for good reason–they ignite conflict.

The Challenge!

No doubt you've received a knock at your front door from well-scrubbed Mormons or Jehovah's Witnesses. Each makes very different claims about God. What are you to think? And how are you to respond when the TV news reports on religious differences that threaten to engulf the world in a nuclear fireball in places like Israel and Kashmir?

Ft. Lauderdale Sun Sentinel published a chilling front-page picture of a twelve-year-old boy taken just seconds before he was shot in Jerusalem. The boy and his father were caught in a crossfire between Palestinian commandos and Israeli police. The photograph captured the sheer terror in the boy's eyes the instant before his death, and illustrated a practical consequence of our different religious beliefs. Palestinians and Israelis fight for many reasons, the most basic of all being that they cannot agree on God.

This same tragedy is repeated around the world: Muslims behead Christians in Indonesia, Sieks kill Hindus in India, and Buddhist monks are murdered by the military dictatorship in Burma. Around the world, blood flows because of disagreements over God.

In response, some like Richard Dawkins and Christopher Hitchens want to dismiss religion altogether as a dangerous relic of the past. Indeed, atheism, small as it is, is growing in America and Europe. But the world has tried life without God. The twentieth century was full of social experiments where men and women tried to govern without God, and it was history's bloodiest one hundred years. Fascists, communists, and secularists all abandoned God only to find themselves no better leaders than the priests and prophets they murdered to replace. The record of history confirms that human beings don't flourish in a godless environment. Indeed, *Time* wrote recently "our brains and bodies contain an awful lot of spiritual wiring." Said another way, we are hard-wired for God.

But whose God are we talking about? Is it the God of the Hindus, the Jews, the Muslims, or the Christians? It cannot be all of them because these different religions claim very different things about God. For example, Muslims claim that there can be no likeness of God on earth, but Christians claim that Jesus was the exact likeness of God on earth. When claims contradict, how do we choose? Political correctness demands tolerance for all religions. We are to live and let live. The common presumption is that "all religions say pretty much the same thing about God so don't sweat the details." But this is not what the different religions themselves say. The Jewish Scripture makes no room for other gods. It does not offer itself as one truth among many. The Old Testament is unyielding.

> I am the Lord, and besides me there is no savior.
>
> *Isaiah 43:11*

> I am the Lord, and *there is no other.*
>
> *Isaiah 45:18*

The most famous tenet of Islam is the Shahadah that claims, "There is no God but Allah, and Mohammad is His prophet." The Baha'i faith contradicts such exclusive claims by declaring each religion to be an expression of spiritual evolution. Such varieties of claims inevitably lead to conflict.

What's a Believer to Do?

Tolerance may be a "sacred" word for urbane twenty-first century residents of New York, Hong Kong, and Dubai, but the New Testament is intolerant of other gods. In fact, Jesus raises the stakes still higher when He says.

> I am the way, the truth, and the life. No one comes to the Father but by me.
>
> *John 14:6*

The exclusive claims of Jesus leave Christians with an uncomfortable choice. World citizenship may demand flexibility, but the world's ancient faiths, and Christianity is particular, are not so easily adaptable.

Recently, I attended a "Christian" interfaith worship service where the cross was removed from the altar and replaced with an enormous picture of the planet earth. My response was mixed. I felt sympathetic to the implied message—that we are all God's children, and as citizens of the world we are responsible for the health and well-being of our planet and its people. But I also sensed a danger of diluting the power of the Christian gospel. Any time the cross of Christ is removed from worship, the core of the Christian message is compromised.

Should followers of Jesus stop reaching out to Jews, Muslims, and Hindus with the gospel's cross when Jesus's own words specifically direct followers to reach out? After all, it was Jesus who said,

> ...go and make disciples of all nations...
>
> *Matthew 28:19*

Presumably "all nations" includes communities and ethnic groups who worship someone or something other than Jesus Christ.

Much of today's tolerance presumes that there is no ultimate truth about God—that one religion is just as valid as another. Math and science can enjoy right and wrong answers, but the subject of God cannot. Indeed, some prefer to keep spiritual things intentionally vague for the sake of peace. But this is not what different religions themselves advocate. Each of the world's major religions stand firm upon their unique claims of Truth. For example: Orthodox Jews don't believe Moses was a myth, and they don't believe that the Ten Commandments are negotiable. They are confident their faith is based upon the facts of history, reason, and revelation.

Muslims believe Mohammed was the true prophet of God, whose sole miracle was reception of the Koran. They believe the Koran to be the literal word of God delivered in God's own language—Arabic. Muslims are confident their beliefs rest upon a reliable/verifiable foundation of history and that their beliefs rest upon facts with right and wrong answers.

Christians are no different. We believe our faith rests upon historical facts that have been confirmed again and again. No serious scholar doubts the historical existence of Jesus, Mary, St. Peter, and St. Paul. Neither do scholars dispute that Jesus died on a Roman cross. The only substantive dispute is with the resurrection. If Jesus remained dead in His tomb, then He was just a man. But if He rose from the dead, well ...He is something else entirely! The study of history presumes that right and wrong answers exist for such historical questions! The resurrection of Jesus must be therefore, either a fact or a fiction.

Today, it is virtually a worldwide creed to believe that human beings are at their core spiritual beings, and to trust that God is at the center of it all. Most believe because they cannot deny the eternity they sense within them. As the Scripture says,

> God " ...has put eternity into man's mind."
>
> *Ecclesiastes 3:11*

But which god is the true God? We are to define God as He is, not as we want Him to be, or as we hope Him to be, or as we presume He should be. The twenty-first century challenge is to define God as God defines Himself.

Is Faith a Blind Leap or an Informed Choice?

For the Christian, the question "Who is God?" is answered "Jesus Christ." The Christian anchors this belief in historical facts, archeological artifacts, and an unequaled collection of preserved first century writings! Far from spiritual mumbo-jumbo, faith in Christ rests on steely facts that have withstood two thousand years of aggressive scrutiny.

It is common to discredit the claims of Christ by highlighting the failures of His followers, and indeed Christians are responsible for many sad and tragic episodes. But the failures of Jesus's followers do not prove Him to be a myth or a humbug. To paraphrase G. K. Chesterton, "Christianity has not been tried and proven false, rather it has been found difficult and proven largely untried."

Jesus lifted the highest moral standard and spiritual vision, so failure by followers should not be a surprise. And even with its past failures, the Christian movement has been the birthplace of schools, universities, hospitals, woman's rights, the championing of the poor, and the elevation of individual worth.

I ask you, which collection of nations has responded most generously to the world's natural disasters and human tragedies? Where have social, economic, and political freedoms made the most progress? Which faith has proved to be the most adaptable to the world's rainbow of cultures? The answer is clear. It is in those countries and cultures where the influence of Jesus Christ has leavened the social life. The impact of Christians and the church upon the world certainly has a mixed record, but the influence of Christ Himself has been remarkably consistent and constructive. Jesus remains largely revered throughout the world even when His church is not.

Christianity all comes down to Jesus. Around the world Jesus is hailed as a prophet, a sage, a holy man of uncommon spiritual power. But there is the thorny issue of His resurrection from the dead. No other spiritual giant makes such an outsized claim for Himself—of being God on earth—and then proving it with a resurrection from the dead. Like I said before, either He did or did not rise from the grave. If He did, and there is considerable evidence that He did, then it is preposterous to call Him anything but Lord. As John Adams once quipped, "Facts are stubborn things."

No Other Gods before Me

At last we come to the First Commandment itself. It is not a politically correct commandment. It is not sensitive to those who do not believe in God. Neither is it tolerant of other religions. It is a flat statement of conviction:

> You shall have no other gods before me.
>
> *Exodus 20:3*

Jews, Muslims, and Christians—roughly half the world's inhabitants—share this commandment. God is to be first in everything we do, in everything we say, and in everything we believe. God is to be above family, country, money, and security. Its application is sobering.

Here, let me illustrate the practical consequence of a daily commitment to the First Commandment. In October 2008, the *New York Times* described the following international scandal on its front page.

> Borepanga India (10/13/08)—The family of Solomon Digal was summoned by neighbors to the public square. They were ordered to get on their knees and bow before the portrait of a Hindu preacher. They were told to turn over their Bibles, hymnals and the other two brightly colored calendar images of Christ that hung on their wall. Then, Mr. Digal, 45, a Christian since childhood, was forced to watch his Hindu neighbors set the items on fire. "Embrace Hinduism and your house will not be demolished. Otherwise, you will be killed, or you will be thrown out of the village." Mr. Digal did what he was told; but even so he and his family were still forced off their farm and out of their village.

It's easy to be glib with the First Commandment, but adhering to it in certain parts of the world can cost you your life. Even a wavering commitment such as Mr. Digal's can be costly. A decision to embrace the First Commandment is the most fundamental of decisions. It determines the orientation and direction of your entire life. So let's review three aspects of the First Commandment that are easy to overlook.

First: What the Command Does Not Say!

Notice what the First Commandment does not say. *It does not say that there are no other gods!* God knows that every human being has the instinct to worship. As Cicero wrote, "The seed of religion is planted in all men." The obvious conclusion is that we will worship something or someone. Scripture cautions:

> Take care, or you *will be* seduced into turning away, serving other gods and worshiping them…
>
> *Deuteronomy 11:16*

Notice how the above verse says "you *will be* seduced into turning away…" It doesn't say you "might be, could be, or possibly will be…" It is a declarative sentence. It says you *will* be. The application is obvious—if you don't worship the one true God, you will be seduced into worshiping a lesser god.

And for those who smugly say to themselves, "But I don't worship any god," beware! Like I said, we are hardwired to worship something be it God, money, success, or pleasure: we all worship something. Here I like G.K. Chesterton's caution, "When people stop believing in God, they don't believe in nothing, they believe in anything."

The ancient people of Israel were most tempted by three particular gods: Baal, the god of sex; Moloch, the god of power and violence; and Mammon, the god of money. In other words, the three gods that the ancient Israelites were most tempted to worship were power, sex, and money. Obviously, things haven't changed very much.

For modern men and women, there is another god that entices our worship—ourselves! We moderns are obsessed with self! We are forever making gods in our own image. Rather than reflecting God, we insist that God reflect ourselves—our values, priorities, and convictions. If God's Bible doesn't agree with our viewpoint, we discredit it. If God's church doesn't support our social agenda, we marginalize it. We have gotten quite comfortable with the notion that we are our own final authority. Many have converted to the secular gospel that proclaims, "God is inside us!"

Sure, you might say to yourself, *I'm too smart for that.* You know better than to succumb to other gods who might entice you. Maybe so, but just keep in mind that someone as wise as Solomon himself was felled by the worship of other gods (1 Kings 11:3).

It is interesting to note that Jesus never once addressed the issue of atheism. He spoke only about the worship of other gods. He knew that deep down there is no such thing as an atheist. Everyone worships something—especially power, sex, and money. So the first thing to note about the First Commandment is that it does not deny the reality of other gods.

Second: Godly Is as Godly Does

Have you noticed that men and women who have been married for a long time seem to look alike? Even if they are of different races, after being married for thirty-seven years, their appearances start to merge! Well, the same principle holds true in our relationship with God. When we worship the Lord over an extended period of time, we start looking like Him—we start to reflect Him. This is why the First Commandment is so uncompromising. God knows that everything is at stake in this one commitment because we become what we worship. God's Word declares that we were created in God's image and that we are to reflect Him first and foremost with our worship. This is what we were created to do—to reflect His image!

James Michener's novel *The Source* describes an ancient pagan family whose father decides to sacrifice his son to his god. The mother grieves while the father performs the ritual sacrifice after which he visits the temple prostitutes. She anguishes over what her husband does in the name of his religion and laments, "With a different god, he would have been a different man." How true. We reflect the god(s) we worship.

Third: "Of Course I Love You... Can You Hold on a Second?"

The First Commandment is emphatic that nothing and no one shall come between you and God. This could be something bad like greed, anger, and egotism. But it could also be something good like a wonderful spouse, a great career, or personal achievement. God's First Commandment demands that nothing, good or bad, come between God and you.

Twenty-six years as a pastor inform me that most people violate the First Commandment, not with something bad but with something good. They don't break the First Commandment by worshiping at the shrine of some pagan god. Instead, they break the commandment with a good thing improperly elevated. Not with a vice but with an overinflated virtue. People rise early for work and come home late without taking time for personal devotion with God. Weekends are crowded with family activities. Sunday morning worship is displaced by little league soccer, a family outing, or catching up on sleep. These may be good, but they are also effective at getting between you and God. It is how the good eclipses the best. Rare is the person who consciously denies God. More often people simply lose touch and drift away.

Of course some folks allow bad things to disrupt their relationship with God. For example, some Jews today still refuse to put God first in their life because of the horror of the holocaust. "How can I put a God first," they reason, "when God allowed such a hideous thing to happen?" And there are others who have had to endure personal tragedy—their child has died, they lost everything in the stock market, their health betrayed them. Such people reject the God who permits such tragedy. Their sorrow and feelings of anger toward God are understandable. But rejecting God doesn't work.

Of course, the most obvious thing that separates us from God is our sin. Publicly, we repudiate sin as a plague. But privately we love our sins, and permit them to drive a wedge between us and God. Different people are drawn to different sins for different reasons. For some, it's pride. For others, it's greed. No matter. Our sins will separate us from God with the speed and efficiency of chemistry. This breaks the Lord's first commandment …and His heart.

The Three-Book Test!

So who or what do you worship? To answer this question I invite you to take what I call the "three-book test," which involves your:

Scheduling book (day timer)
Checkbook
Good Book (Bible)

Scheduling Book: "Are You Free Next Week, God?"

First, take out your scheduling book or device (Blackberry or iPhone) and review how you spend your time. Nothing is more precious than your time, and how you spend it testifies to your priorities. For example: If you don't spend time with your spouse, sooner or later he/she will feel neglected. My wife and I have an understanding that each evening I will devote fifteen minutes of undivided attention to her. I will sit beside her, look directly into her eyes, and without any distractions focus on her.

This same principle holds true in a relationship with God. If you don't spend time with God, your soul will eventually feel neglected! God wants to bless you, but if His presence in your life is eclipsed because you are busy chasing other gods, your soul will not thrive. The Scriptures offer this promise to those who put God first.

> In everything you do, put God first and He will direct you and crown your efforts with success.
>
> *Proverbs* 3:6 (LB)

The most precious thing you can give to God is your time. He wants to occupy first place in your schedule. This is a reason why the earliest church chose to gather for worship early in the morning on the *first day of the week.* The early church intentionally gave their first and best time to God. Worship is how they began their week.

Today, Sunday morning feels like the end of the line—the time to recover in bed from what happened the week before. But in theory, Sunday morning worship is to be the start of the week. In it we bring to God the best that we have in time, attention, praise, money, and service. Sunday is when we give Him our first and our best.

The Checkbook: Money, Money, Money!

The second way to test the priority of God in your life is by opening your checkbook. Jesus said, "Where your treasure is, there will your heart be." In other words, the heart follows the money. It's not the money that follows the heart. So, based on your checkbook, where does God stand? Is He number one? The Bible is clear that you are to give 10 percent to God's work in the world. The giving of 10 percent is intended to teach you to put God first. The Bible says:

> The purpose of tithing is to teach you to put God first...
>
> *Deuteronomy* 14:23 (LB)

God wants to bless you, but it's hard if you won't trust Him with your money. He wants to give Himself to you, but you may not be willing because you're too busy clutching something else. The old expression of "let go and let God" is appropriate here. Until you are willing to let go of control (money being the biggest control issue there is) you are not going to be able to submit yourself to the direction and blessing of God.

The Good Book: Blessed Are the Readers!

The third test is the Good Book—your devotion. To determine God's place in your life, review the time spent with your Bible. After all, if you really want to hear from God, why not start with His Word? A relationship with God requires time and effort. There are no spiritual shortcuts. You can't offer God a second-class effort and expect a first-class blessing. God wants to bless you far beyond your wildest dreams, but you must put Him first, which requires that you spend time with Him in His Word!

As a pastor I've visited thousands of people in their homes. Often there will be a huge family Bible sitting prominently on the living room table as a proud family heirloom. But it's equally obvious that the book hasn't been read. In truth, it functions more like a family good luck charm than a spiritual tool to connect the family with God.

To summarize, the Lord wants you to:

- Read His Word,
- Give your money, and
- Devote your time to Him.

There are no spiritual shortcuts! To put God first in your life, and to honor both the letter and the spirit of the First Commandment, concrete steps must be taken. God is no one's fool. He knows the truth of your commitment to Him. And the surest way to know the truth yourself is by taking the "three-book test."

Conclusion

At the start of the twentieth century, three of the world's most influential thinkers wrote that God did not exist. Fredrick Nietzsche, the philosopher, claimed God was dead. Karl Marx, the political scientist, maintained that religion and God were merely the opiate of the people. And Sigmund Freud, the psychiatrist, complained that God was nothing more than a neurotic projection of the human subconscious. As the twentieth century unfolded, much blood and treasure was dedicated to deciding God's existence. Indeed, more people were murdered during the 20th century than in all other centuries combined, due to men like Hitler, Stalin, Mao, and Pol Pot who were convinced that there was no God.

But at the start of the twenty-first century, most of the world has concluded that God does in fact exist. Never before has belief in God spread more dynamically than now. But we are still left with a huge question, "Whose God are we talking about?"

The truth staked out by the First Commandment is this—at the final judgment you will have only one God to stand before. The Scriptures are clear that heaven is a place for those whose priority is God. After all, a person for whom God wasn't their priority wouldn't enjoy heaven, for heaven is all about God. And for Christians, this God is revealed in Jesus Christ.

But what if God hasn't been your first priority? Do you still have hope? The good news of the gospel is that anytime is a good time to make God number one in your life. You only need to open you heart to Him. You don't have to pay Him back for past sins, square away your present circumstances, or have your future all figured out. You only need to open your heart right now and allow Him to occupy its first and most important place. When you do this, you will discover that God is much better than you ever dreamed. He is eager to forgive any sin you confess. He wants to help you live the kind of abundant life for which you've always hoped. He will astonish you with His generosity, amaze you with His sensitivity, and confound you with His ability to lead you through whatever trial and tribulation you might be facing.

God wants to be number one in your life so that you can be number one in His heart. There is nothing He won't do for your sake. Indeed, He was willing to die on a cross for you. In return He invites you to make Him number one, to worship Him and Him alone, and He promises to surprise you with joy. This is the first of His Ten Commandments!

To conclude, some would have us homogenize the different world religions into a bland and unthreatening bowl of spiritual mush. But this is not an option the First Commandment offers. It insists upon a choice—to receive or reject the God of Abraham, Isaac, and Jacob ...the God of the Virgin Mary and the Apostle Paul. To finesse this command by linking it with the gods of other religions is to do injustice to the blunt force of its intended meaning. The First Commandment recognizes that there are many spiritual choices for many different people, but only one God. As His Word proclaims:

> I know that the Lord is great, that our Lord is greater than all gods.
>
> *Psalm 135:5*

Study Guide: My God Is Bigger Than Your God.

90 Minutes

Introduction (10 minutes)

Briefly

Have each participant introduce themselves by name and have them share which of the Ten Commandments they find easiest to obey and why.

Opening Discussion/Warm Up (15 minutes)

Share an encounter you had with someone who expressed a different understanding of who God is (i.e., Buddhist, Muslim, or Mormon), and using one sentence describe:

what it makes you think, and
how it caused you to feel.

Who Is God? (20 minutes)

The fastest-growing religion in Asia, Africa, and South America is Christianity. The fastest-growing religion in Europe is Islam. And the fastest-growing religion in America is secularism. Do you think these shifts will cause more or less tension over the next fifty years? Have you personally experienced any of this tension?

Isaiah 41–45 includes a courtroom scene, where God invites us (Isaiah 41:21) to put His identity on trial.

Is God tolerant of other gods? (Isaiah 43:11–13)

Who are the witnesses in this trial? (Isaiah 43:10)

Can human beings thwart God's purposes? (Isaiah 43:13)

What is the final verdict of God's trial? (Isaiah 45:21)

What is good about the current culture of tolerance? What is bad about it?

Is the God of the Bible tolerant of other gods? (Isaiah 45:18–21)

According to John 14:6, did Jesus consider Himself to be "*a* savior" or "*the* savior?"

In today's pluralistic world culture how "inconvenient" is this exclusive claim of Jesus?

How do you answer when you are accused of being intolerant because of your Christian practice?

No Other Gods ... (10 minutes)

Read out loud the First Commandment together.

Break into groups of three.

Before you became a Christian, to what did you bow down?

Is there something to which you currently struggle to resist bowing down?

Can good things (family and career) be as effective as bad things (selfishness and fear) in getting between yourself and God? Do "good" things get between you and God?

The seven deadly sins are: pride, greed, anger, lust, envy, gluttony, and sloth. Do these sins eclipse God *against our will?*

The Three Book Test (20 minutes)

Stay in your group of three.

What does your scheduling book (day timer), your checkbook, and your Good Book (Bible) say about how you observe the First Commandment?

What do you do each day to spend time with God?

Do you tithe 10 percent of your income to God? What is your biggest fear in doing (or not doing) this?

Pick a time this week when you will read your Bible.

Write down your plans for your upcoming week, and share them with your group.

Wrap Up (15 minutes)

Gather together.

Offer a short discussion on praying for others.

Share your prayer requests with one another.

Confirm the date and location of the next meeting.

Close by reading out loud the following prayer:

Dear God,

We thank You for bringing us together to study Your Word, to share fellowship, and to encourage one another!

We confess that You have not always been our first love. We have chased after and bowed down to other gods who have enticed us. We have allowed difficult circumstances to frighten us into seeking help from people, places, and things that are unhealthy and unfaithful. We have allowed our time, attention, and treasure to focus on inferior practices. Even so, Lord, we come now to re–dedicate ourselves. You are our God, our Lord, and our Master. You are the One who gave us life in our mother's womb, and You are the one who breathed life into our spirit. May we hold You close to our hearts as You hold each of us close to Yours. And bless our fellowship, Lord. May we take the time and make the effort to know the concerns of each member of our group, and to act where we can. May our fellowship be a blessing to each as we encourage one another to draw closer to You. Amen.

Command Two:
Sometimes It Feels Good to Smash Things!

Several years ago my newly married neighbors got into a terrible shouting match in their kitchen. The argument quickly escalated, whereupon the wife lost all composure, opened up the cupboard over the stove, and started firing china at her husband. Her throws pinned the poor man against a kitchen wall as she reached for plates, coffee cups, and saucers—one right after the other smashing against the wall as her flabbergasted husband ducked this way and that to avoid them. Shards of china flew everywhere as she emptied out her frustration. The whole thing was so absurd they both got to laughing. When the cupboard was finally empty, her bemused husband asked, "Are you all right?" To which his wife answered with a satisfied smile, "I feel great!"

Yep, sometimes it can feel good to smash something! It has to do with all the pent up emotion that builds up inside. Let me be clear, I don't recommend smashing china as an approach to conflict resolution. But there are moments when all the dammed-up emotion demands expression, and smashing something can help break the tension. Indeed, in San Diego, California, there is a little shop called Sarah's Smash Shack, which was the subject of a National Public Radio broadcast not long ago (Oct. 10, 2008).

Apparently Sarah tapped into this phenomenon of smashing plates to relieve tension. At her smash shack $45 would buy you the opportunity to hurl fifteen full-size plates against a concrete wall. According to the NPR feature, business was brisk.

This chapter is intended to smash something. It is to smash all the idols we worship that frustrate our lives, twist our emotions, and ruin our walk with God. This is what the Second Commandment is all about—smashing idols. It says:

> Do not bow down to any idol or worship it, because I am the Lord your God and I tolerate no rivals…
>
> *Exodus* 20:5 (GN)

Here the Bible tells us in plain words that the Lord does not tolerate any idol that would rival Him. You are not to fashion or bow down to any image that attempts to represent Him, or any other god. There is nothing subtle about this commandment. No idols—period.

The Second Commandment is also the only one of the ten that offers *both* a blessing and a curse.

Curse:

> …I bring punishment on those who hate me…
>
> *Exodus* 20:5 (GN)

Blessing:

> But I show my love …to those who love me and obey my laws.
>
> *Exodus* 20:6 (GN)

How does God view idolatry? According to Exodus 20:5, God experiences idol worship as hatred toward Him. Whether or not we intend idol worship to be hatred makes no difference. Hatred is the way God experiences it. It is a simple matter of jealousy.

God admits as much in the Second Commandment. He says, " ...for I the Lord your God am a jealous God..."

When Stephanie and I first got married, I still had pictures of my old girlfriends in some of my photo albums. When she came across them, she was offended. She wanted to know why I still had them ...Did I miss them? Did I still have any lingering emotional attachments to them? Her hurt soon turned to jealous anger, and our china came close to flying. Now, take the jealousy of my wife and multiply it—this is what you have when God discovers that you have a secret love ...an image or idol that you secretly adore. Hell hath no fury like the scorn of our jealous God. By the way, being a quick study, I burned the offending photos. Idols demand the same treatment. We are to burn them, smash them, and rid them from our lives forever.

Let's look at the example of someone who did just that.

King Josiah: Idol Smasher

The Old Testament tells the story of Josiah, a young Hebrew King who was crowned as a boy at a time of crippling national corruption. His people worshiped all sorts of idols, images, and foreign gods, and allowed Jerusalem's temple to fall into disrepair. So far had the Israelites fallen spiritually that even the very laws of Moses had been lost! Imagine, *losing* the laws of Moses! But Josiah grew into a remarkable young man who feared the Lord and who had a heart for being faithful.

When Josiah was twenty-six years old, he ordered the temple repaired and orthodox worship restored. During the repair, his carpenters and stonemasons uncovered the Books of Moses. Josiah read them and was convicted by how far he and his people had fallen. He then made the decision to smash every image and idol of a foreign god. Here is how the Scripture describes Josiah's approach:

> The king (Josiah) smashed all the altars to smithereens—he smashed them all, pulverized the fragments, and scattered their dust in the Valley of Kidron. The King proceeded to make a clean sweep of all the sex-and-religion shrines that had proliferated ...He tore apart the altars, chopped down the phallic Asherah-poles, and scattered old bones over the sites ...Josiah scrubbed the place clean and trashed spirit-mediums, sorcerers, domestic gods, and carved figures—all the vast accumulation of foul and obscene relics and images on display everywhere ...Josiah did this in obedience to the words of God's Revelation ... found in the Temple of God. There was no king to compare with Josiah ...who turned in total and repentant obedience to God.
>
> *2 Kings 23:12 (The Message)*

It's time to follow Josiah's example and smash the idols that keep us from God. We may not bow down to golden calves, but we do bow down regularly to the images that glow from our televisions sets: success, power, sensuality. It's time to smash these idols, just as King Josiah did. But what would this look like? Just what does the Second Commandment demand?

Universal Principle

The Ten Commandments are laws about which Jews, Muslims, and Christians largely agree. What's more, the Second Commandment also enjoys agreement with other world religions. For example: Buddhist scripture says:

> Who sees me by form, who seeks me in sound, Perverted are his footsteps upon the way.
>
> *Diamond Sutra, 26*

Buddha directs us not to look for God in the things of the world. He considered the physical world with its desires and striving an illusion. He counseled not to worship the creation! Indeed, the Second Commandment enjoys a wide consensus among the world's major religions. But if one were asked, "Do you have a problem bowing down to graven images and worshiping idols?" I doubt many would say, "Yes, that's just my problem!" Most civilized people presume they are above the concern expressed in the Second Commandment. Yet the Bible cautions that the Second Command was the very first of the Ten Commandments broken. Even before Moses could descend from Mount Sinai with the Ten Commandments the Israelite people had already fashioned a golden calf to worship. But once he saw it, Moses lost all composure.

> He took the bull-calf which they had made, melted it, ground it into fine powder, and mixed it with water. Then he made the people of Israel drink it.
>
> *Exodus* 32:20 (GN)

Moses smashed an idol that day!

It's doubtful you bow down to anything like a golden calf today, but there are images to which you're vulnerable—images of success, status, wealth, power, and sensuality. These are today's idols. And the altar where they are worshiped is your television and computer. Each day you turn on your television where in these images turn you on—enticing you to buy them, pursue them, work for them, compromise for them, borrow for them, and basically sell your soul for them. It has been said that your god is whatever controls you. If that is so then there can be no doubt that the images pouring out of that bluish glow from your television and computer are the gods of your life.

I know of one courageous young mother named Dorothy who took a sledgehammer to her family television. Dorothy's husband, Dan, an attorney, loved to come home after work and park himself in front of the TV. When he did, he tuned out everything and everyone around him. One evening, however, their son needed help with his homework, but each time he approached his dad, he only got a grunt, as his dad stared blankly into the tube. Well, after watching their son try unsuccessfully several times to get his father's attention, Dorothy's pent-up frustration snapped. She marched to the garage, grabbed the sledgehammer, and proceeded to smash the family television to bits. Dan sat in his chair incredulous as Dorothy vented her fury. It was an expensive lesson, but one that did grab Dan's attention. He gave his son all the help he needed.

The Bible is absolutely clear in its prohibition of worshiping idols and images. It says:

> *For your own good* ...do not sin by making ...an idol in any form at all.
>
> *Deut.* 4:15–16 (GN)

Notice how God emphasizes, "For your own good..." God doesn't prescribe the second commandment because He is insecure about His place in your life—that if you don't worship Him He will feel somehow diminished. He gives this commandment for your own good. God insists on being first because it is good for you. For when God is first, all other priorities naturally fall into proper order.

What Happens When We Worship Images?

Keep in mind that the images and idols that the world offers usually promise more than they can deliver. Television commercials promise that to brush with certain toothpaste will make your smile irresistible, drive a certain car and you will achieve enviable status, or drink a particular beer and you'll be a real man. It's time to smash such images. The Bible says:

> Those who make idols are disillusioned...
>
> *Jeremiah* 10:14 (GN)

How many times must we buy into the world's lies, only to be disillusioned? The Scripture goes on to say:

> [Before you knew Christ] you were controlled by dead idols, who always lead you astray.
>
> 1 *Corinthians* 12:2 (TEV)

Let me ask you a personal question: Who or what controls you? Are you controlled by an ideal image of what you are supposed to weigh, by a vision of the kind of lifestyle and status you are supposed to enjoy, or by the dream and hunger for a particular kind of love and romance? What controls you? Many today are mortgaged up to their eyeballs with multiple credit cards maxed out. Bill collectors know their phone numbers by heart. They're working horrendous hours ...Why? To pay for an image presumed necessary for happiness. It's time to smash these idols of success, beauty, and status that have all but ruined us!

Scripture emphasizes that you were created in the image of God! But the Bible also goes on to say,

> Those who make idols will become like them...
>
> *Psalm* 115:8, *paraphrase*

A basic spiritual principle is this: "you become what you worship/idolize." You might worship success and indeed become successful. But success doesn't guarantee a satisfying marriage and a happy home. Success doesn't promise well-adjusted children and a joyful collection of friends and neighbors. Success as the world today defines it breeds obsessive work, a competitive spirit, and a limited personal life. Success today is more image than reality.

Several years ago my older sister worked for a photographic retouching firm in New York City. What her firm did was to retouch high fashion photos of models intended for magazines like *Cosmopolitan* and *Vogue*. If a model had a skin flaw that showed up on the photo, they would simply airbrush it out. But they could also do more. They could actually manipulate the model's picture, taking a bit off the waist and enhancing here and there. In other words, the images published in *Vogue* and *Cosmo* are not real. Think of all the men and women who disfigure themselves with plastic surgery, implants, injections, and tummy tucks to match these images even though they are not real! These are images that need to be smashed.

No Idols of God

The Second Commandment not only prohibits making idols, but it also prohibits making any image of God. God directs us not to worship anything that represents Him:

> You shall not make for yourself an idol in the form of anything in heaven…
>
> *Exodus* 20:5

We are not to make any image or likeness of God because it only serves to shrink His stature. As magnificent and inspiring as Michelangelo's painted images of God are in the Sistine Chapel, still, they limit our understanding of who God is and what He does. With the Second Commandment God specifically prohibits this!

But here we can get into some difficult debate.

In 2001 the Taliban of Afghanistan decided to dynamite the Bamyan Buddha, a one hundred eighty-foot statue carved into a mountainside during the sixth century AD because Islamic Sharia law forbids idols. World opinion was outraged. The statue of Buddha was an international treasure, a priceless piece of our human cultural history. But the Taliban ignored the international outcry and lit the dynamite to cries of "Allah Akbar!" ("God is great!")

No reasonable world citizen would accept a cultural atrocity like sandblasting Michelangelo's frescos off the walls of the Sistine Chapel or blowing up the temples at Angkor Wat in Cambodia in the name of the Second Commandment! Those are precious treasures of cultural history, yet many sincere believers see them as idols.

There is no consensus in the Christian world regarding the application of the Second Commandment. Catholic, Orthodox, and Episcopal churches are heavy laden with icons, frescos, and statues. Mennonite churches are unadorned, sparse, with whitewashed walls. What might resolve this tension is the perspective that it is not wood or stone but the heart that makes an idol. God does not abhor the material we fashion into art. It is our hearts that get us into trouble.

In the book of Exodus, God reveals Himself to be a prolific artist, where He gives explicit instruction for how to build His holy tabernacle festooned with images of angels and cherubs, heaven, and nature. With His tabernacle and later the holy temple of Jerusalem God shows Himself to be an outrageously creative and sensual artist, so it would seem logical to deduce that the Second Commandment is not a prohibition against artistry and creativity. Rather it is a prohibition against bowing down to the creativity. Clearly, we are to worship the Creator, not our own creation!

Why Do We Create Idols?

So why do we create and worship idols? Well, we all have an instinctual need to worship something. There is a God consciousness built into every human heart that needs expression. Throughout recorded history, and in every culture, someone or something is worshiped. So why have we insisted on worshiping images and idols of our own creation, instead of the living God? The answers are many. Let me offer three.

First, when you make your own god, then you are your own lord and master. You're not submitted to any God who would tell you what to do. You prefer a god who can be manipulated—one who will do what you want. The best way to insure this is to worship a god of your own making.

A second reason is to limit God's presence. To make God a thing—a statue, a sacred object—is to put limits on where God can be. He is no longer everywhere, which means of course that He can no longer see and judge everything. With God confined to an object your actions are hidden from His scrutiny. You limit God's reach.

A third reason to worship a god of your own making is to limit God's power. Most people prefer a tame god, one who can be shaped to suit their wants and interests. In other words, many want just enough of a god to bless them, but not enough of a god to challenge them. Really, what most people want is a genie, someone who exists to grant wishes, rather than a God who calls lives into account.

Let me share the following story that illustrates why we worship idols that we can manipulate.

There was once a boy who wanted a bike for Christmas, and so he decided to write a letter to Jesus to ask for help in securing his bike. He began his letter, "Dear Jesus, I've been a really good boy this year, and I would really like your help…" But he tore up the letter because he knew it wasn't true. He tried again, "Dear Jesus, I've tried really hard to be a good boy…" But he knew that this wasn't right either, so he tried again, "Dear Jesus, I would like to be a good boy…" But again he knew this too rang hollow. Suddenly he hit upon an inspiration. He ran to the living room, grabbed the statue of Virgin Mary, wrapped it in a towel and hid it under his bed and then wrote, "Dear Jesus, if you ever want to see your mother again…"

It's tempting to limit god to something we can control and manipulate. Honestly, a genie is closer to what is wanted—someone who will grant us our wishes ...who will get us what we want. But it's time to smash such idols so we can be free to worship the one and true God.

The Benefits of Worshiping Only God

The Second Commandment is all about smashing the false images and idols you worship, and *how good that can make you feel!*

I'll never forget the day the Berlin Wall fell in 1989. Experts expressed fear that the wall's fall would destabilize the world, and that war could follow. Instead there was open rejoicing on both sides of the divide. People on both sides stuck their hands through holes to shake hands. Young men and women danced and embraced atop the concrete partition. Television crews beamed video around the world of men and women taking sledgehammers to the wall and bashing it into chunks of rubble. The euphoria was contagious. It was a spectacular instance of how good it can feel to take a sledgehammer to something that needs to be smashed.

There are many idols and images that you and I need to smash today. The pervasive worship of power, sex, and money are the most obvious candidates. Such idols need to be smashed if ever we are to be filled with God.

The New Testament tells of how Jesus took to smashing things. It occurred right after He rode into Jerusalem on Palm Sunday. The city was euphoric. Expectations for God to do something great were at a fever pitch. And the Lord did do something, but it wasn't what the crowds expected. For after the Palm Sunday parade Jesus made His way to the temple. And there, seeing all the buying and selling going on in a holy place He was filled with zealous anger. John tells us,

> And making a whip of cords, he drove them all, with the sheep and oxen, out of the temple; and he poured out the coins of the money changers and overturned their tables.
>
> *John* 2:15 *(*RSV*)*

Here we have an illustration of Jesus smashing idols in the temple court …idols we still bow down to today—money, power, success. Jesus took a whip of cords to it all and smashed everything in sight.

Conclusion:

To follow Christ is to do the same. It is to free oneself from the things that obscure God, such as: public opinion, peer pressure, keeping up with the Joneses, and the need for all our status and stuff. We are to smash it all and watch the shattered pieces fly every which way. You'll be amazed at just how good you feel after you've done it. Indeed, you'll feel tensions broken, burdens lifted, and the pressure relieved! You'll feel just great! In fact, remember Sara's Smash Shack at this chapter's beginning? You might want to visit and celebrate a little bit by and letting a couple of plates fly. Amen.

Study Guide: Sometimes It Feels Good to Smash Things!

90 Minutes

Introduction (10 Minutes)

Briefly

Have each participant share their name and a story in which something was smashed in a fit of tension/frustration.

Universal Principle: (20 minutes)

In what ways are the images of success, status, wealth, power, and sensuality worshiped today?

It has been said that "your god is whatever controls you." Turn to a partner and share one-on-one what your date book (how your time is spent) and checkbook (how your money is spent) would reveal who or what controls you.

What Happens When We Worship Images? (15 minutes)

The Bible says:

> (Before you knew Christ) you were controlled by dead idols, who always lead you astray.
>
> 1 *Corinthians* 12:2 (TEV)

Assign each of the four corners of your room to a particular idol: money, power, appearance, pleasure. Have each of the participants go to the corner that represents the idol that controlled them before they met Christ. Have them share amongst themselves stories of how their idol controlled them.

There is a spiritual principle that says that "we become like what we worship." Was that true for you? Did you become like the thing your worshiped?

No Idols of God! (10 minutes)

Does the Second Commandment imply that we are not to employ our artistic talents in the worship of God? What would a Catholic or Episcopalian say? What would an old order Mennonite say?

In the book of Exodus (chapters 37–39) doesn't God direct the Israelites to be artistically creative and expressive ...enlisting art for the sake of worship?

Why Do We Create Idols? (10 minutes)

When you make your own god, are you still in control?

When you make your own god, do you limit your god's presence and power?

The Benefits of Worshiping Only God (20 minutes)

The benefit of worshiping God is that we become like Him!

> As the Spirit of the Lord works within us, we become more and more like Him.
>
> *2 Corinthians* 3:18 (LB)

Share with the group what evidence you have of this being true in your life.

Wrap Up(5 minutes)

Share your prayer requests with one another.

Confirm the date and location of the next meeting.

Close by reading out loud the following prayer.

Prayer:

Lord, You know our every weakness. You know the images that entice us ...the many little gods that compete for our attention and worship. We pray, Lord, that You help us to smash them all. May nothing eclipse our relationship with You, Lord! Amen.

Command Three:
God's Last Name Isn't "Damn"!

A twenty-two-year-old single woman recently had her name changed in Las Vegas! In front of television millions, her name changed from Caressa Cameron to Miss America, and her life will never be the same! Why? Because a name can mean everything!

Shakespeare said as much in his drama of Romeo and Juliet. In his play's most famous scene, Juliet leans from her balcony and asks herself, "What is in a name?" and by the play's end, she learns that her name will cost her life!

In different parts of the globe, you can live as neighbors, drink from the same well, vote in the same elections, and share the same government, but the consequences of your name being Palestinian or Israeli, Sunni or Shiite, male or female can mean very different lives!

In business, the name of your company is a life-and-death concern. Coca-Cola spends millions of advertising dollars to uphold its name before the public. TV sponsors during the Super Bowl pay a fortune for just thirty seconds of commercial time all because a good name will make or break their business.

In American politics if you have the last name of Kennedy in Massachusetts or Bush in Texas, you are likely to do well. In banking if you have the last name Rothschild or Rockefeller, you are likely to do well. And in sports, if you have the last name Manning advertisers will be eager to associate with you.

What is in a name? Well, a good name can mean everything, which brings us to God's Third Commandment.

> You shall not misuse the *name* of the Lord your God, for the Lord will not hold anyone guiltless who misuses His name.
>
> *Exodus* 20:7

God knows the value of a good name, and for this reason He expects His name honored above every other.

God's Name

The Bible employs over three hundred names for God such as Elohim "Faithful One" and El-Shaddai "God Almighty." Then there are the nonbiblical names for God, such as "the Man upstairs" and "the great eye in the sky." But there is only one name that God specifically chose for Himself—Yahweh "I am." Let me share the story of God choosing this strange name for Himself found in Exodus 3 and 4.

Forty years after Moses escaped Pharaoh's death threat in Egypt, Moses was shepherding the sheep of his father-in-law Jethro at the foot of Mt. Sinai. One day Moses saw a strange wonder, a burning bush that was not consumed …He climbed to investigate, and as he drew near, Moses heard God's voice out of the bush's flames.

"Moses, put off thy shoes …for the place whereon you stand is holy ground."

God then directed Moses to return to Egypt to rescue the Hebrew people from their bitter slavery to Pharaoh. But Moses objected. He felt inadequate, believing no one would take him seriously. After all, he didn't even know God's name. So Moses asked God, "What shall I say to the people of Israel when they ask what your name is?"

To which God answered, "I AM who I AM …tell them that I AM sent you."

This is the strange name God chose for Himself—"I AM"—Yahweh. (Significantly, the ancient Hebrew language has no past or future tense, only a present. Past and future in the Hebrew language are determined by context. At the risk of oversimplifying the Hebrew, the name Yahweh [I am] also means "I Was" and "I Will Be." In other words, God names Himself I Was, I Am, I Will Be. God's name, therefore, declares Him to be the One who exists forever.)

God Is Sensitive about His Name

The Third Commandment emphasizes an essential spiritual principle. It is this: God is sensitive about His name. This sensitivity is echoed throughout scripture. For example, in the book of Leviticus we read the story of a young man who made the mistake of misusing God's name.

> One day the son of an Israelite mother and an Egyptian father went out among the Israelites. A fight broke out in the camp between him and an Israelite. The son of the Israelite woman blasphemed the Name of God and cursed. They brought him to Moses. His mother's name was Shelomith, daughter of Dibri of the tribe of Dan. They put him in custody waiting for God's will to be revealed to them.
>
> Then God spoke to Moses: "Take the blasphemer outside the camp. Have all those who heard him place their hands on his head; then have the entire congregation stone him. Then tell the Israelites, anyone who curses God will be held accountable; anyone who blasphemes the

> Name of God must be put to death. The entire congregation must stone him. It makes no difference whether he is a foreigner or a native, if he blasphemes the name, he will be put to death."
>
> *Lev.* 24:10–16 *(The Message)*

Obviously, God does not consider His name anything to be used casually, disrespectfully, or meaninglessly.

But why is God so sensitive? Is He insecure? Is God like the schoolyard boy named "Beauregard" who hates being teased by classmates about his name? Or is God somehow insulted by a profane abuse of His name? Why out of Ten Commandments would God elevate honoring His name to third on His list?

Please note that Jesus also expressed sensitivity for God's name. He began His Lord's Prayer with the words: "Our Father, who art in heaven, *hallowed be thy name.*" So why this sensitivity for God's name? Let me share three reasons:

First, the importance of meaning: We moderns are quite casual with cuss'n. It is considered a harmless offense to swear using the Lord's name. But this blasé attitude disconnects us from a larger truth. Loose use of God's name quite effectively renders it meaningless, and God is sensitive to this. He wants His name to mean something—certainly more than a meaningless profanity! In His name there is life, healing, and hope, so we are commanded to reverence it.

So why do people cuss using the Lord's name? Well, mostly for effect. Folks try to appear strong by using strong language. But any fool can cuss. It requires no intellect, courage, or creativity. Swearing is nothing but weak people using strong words … or more accurately—empty words. To swear is to empty God's name of its meaning, and God takes this personally. He considers it more than impolite; He considers it immoral.

Another meaningless use of God's name is when we *impulsively* blurt out God's name to express surprise or excitement.

For example, we see a moving car nearly hit a child and we blurt out—"Oh my God!"—reducing God's name to a mere exclamation point. Of course, most people would say, "Yes, but when I say it I really don't mean anything by it." That's just the point! We reduce God's holy name to nothing! A name which the ancient saints trembled to speak we now employ carelessly. In the Gospel of Matthew, Jesus cautions,

> ...Every idle word that men shall speak, they shall give account thereof in the day of judgment.
>
> *Matthew* 12:36 *(*KJV*)*

Even if we don't take the Lord's name seriously, God still does, and He will hold us accountable.

Second, the importance of character: A name establishes *character,* and to misuse God's name is to slander God's character. Allow me a simple illustration.

The most popular boy's name in America today is Michael. By itself the name says nothing about character. But add to Michael the last name Jordan or Tyson and immediately two very different characters come to mind.

Listen carefully! God's last name is not "Damn"! People use the God with damn expression all the time, and God takes this offense seriously. Why? Because it slanders His character by suggesting that God damns people, when God's purpose is just the opposite. As the Scripture says, God comes...

> ...not to condemn the world, but that the world might be saved through Him.
>
> *John* 3:17

God is forever trying to rescue people, so to use the "God with damn" expression slanders God by suggesting He has a judgmental character. Tragically, the only thing some folks know about

God is that His name is used to condemn them. So you see it's not that God is insecure, or that God finds the profane use of His name insulting. Just the opposite. God is sensitive to the abuse of His name because He knows profaning it misrepresents Him, which can close people off to His blessing.It is not God's pleasure to damn anyone. As the Scripture says:

> the Lord is …not wanting anyone to perish…
>
> 2 *Peter* 3:9

Third, the importance of authority: God takes the commandment to honor His name seriously because a name establishes *authority.*

The names Washington, Jefferson, Lincoln, Roosevelt, and now Obama carry great authority in America. These names are referenced in speeches, articles, and books not only for their history, but also for their political authority. The same is true with God. God's name is used to reference His spiritual and moral authority. Unfortunately, too often it is misused for self-serving ends. The Third Commandment specifically prohibits manipulating God's name for our own purposes. Let me give a specific example.

The Third Commandment prohibits the misuse of God's name. To leverage His name to promote self-serving ends is just such an abuse. Some of what is done in God's name has nothing to do with God. His name is to be reserved for His agenda, not our own. In American politics over the past thirty years, the Republican party has leveraged the name of God to advance their political agenda—by securing the "values vote." (The Democratic party probably would have done the same thing if they had the opportunity.) This is a misuse of God's name. Because of the self-serving way God's name has been leveraged in politics, many now want nothing to do with God.

According to pollster George Barna, 66 percent of Americans admit to misusing the Lord's name. I'm sure that many, if not most, had no idea that God took the misuse of His name so gravely. But think of it, if anyone on national television were to refer to President Obama using the "n-word" reaction would be swift and crushing. There would be zero tolerance. Why then would we presume that God would be any less offended when we misuse or disrespect His name?

The Promise and Blessing of God's Name

On the positive side, the Bible contains verse after verse that blesses those who honor and reverence the name of God. The Scripture says,

> You (God) have given me the blessing you reserve for those who reverence your *name.*
>
> *Psalm* 61:5 *(*LB*)*

Here are more examples:

> Security— "The *name* of the Lord is a strong tower; the righteous run to it and are safe."
>
> *(Proverbs* 18:10*)*

> Help— "Our help is in the *name* of the Lord."
>
> *(Psalm* 124:8*)*

> Gladness— "In Him our hearts rejoice, for we trust in his holy *name.*"
>
> *(Psalm* 33:21*)*

> Salvation— "Everyone who calls on the *name* of the Lord will be saved."
>
> *(Romans* 10:13*)*

> Promise— "Ask anything, using my *name*, and I will do it!" *(John* 14:14, LB*)*

These are the promises offered to those who reverence the name of the Lord and call upon His name.

Using God's Name Correctly

So then how do we use God's name correctly? We get a clue in the Lord's Prayer.

The Lord's Prayer instructs us to honor the name of God when it says, "Our Father, who art in heaven, *hallowed be thy name.*" The word "hallowed" means holy. We are to treat the name of God with "holiness," which means *to set apart.* The name of God is to be set apart from every other name. We are to treat it as sacred.

In ancient Israel, the priests took the name of God so seriously that they would not even speak it. As ancient scribes wrote copies of the Bible, when they came the name of God, they would put down their pen, rise, bathe, put on clean garments, take a pen that had never been used before, and only then write down the name of God. Some of us might think this excessive, but the Scripture is absolutely clear that we are to honor the name of God with all that we say, do, think, and feel.

You might say to yourself, *Well, the Third Commandment is just not that important to me.* Maybe so, but evidently it is to God. It is serious enough for God to instruct Moses to stone to death anyone who blasphemed His name.

Our speech is to be consistent at work, at the ball field, at home, and at church. Integrity means living by a single high standard where our deeds match our creeds. Our words are to reflect our worship. We are to respect and honor the name of God where at all times and in all places.

I read an article recently by a father who said that the single worst moment of his life was when he heard his three-year-old son say "dammit." Shocked, the father turned to the boy and asked, "Where did you learn that?" To which the son answered innocently, "From you, Dad." The number one place we have to work on our mouths is at home. Verbal misuse and abuse is rampant, and if it is going to stop, it has got to start in our homes.

A survey taken at the University of Chicago asked graduate students where they got most of their ideas about morality and religion. The majority said, "Through conversation with the family at mealtimes."

The way we reverence God (or don't reverence God) at home has a tremendous impact on our children. They listen to everything we say, and they will grow up either believing that "Damn" is God's last name, or believing that the name of God is a source of blessing and reverence.

Conclusion

The trouble most of us have with God's Third Commandment is not with the words we choose. Our words reflect what resides within our hearts. We can wash our mouths out with soap, but that will never get at the real problem. The problem is the heart. Whatever is in our hearts is going to come out in our speech, especially when the pressure is on. We are like a tube of toothpaste. Whatever we're full of comes out when the squeeze is on. If our hearts are full of anger, jealousy, despair, anxiety, or fear, it is going to come out in what we say when the pressure is on. Swearing and disrespecting the name of God is just a symptom of the turmoil in our hearts. Luke 6:45 says,

> It is out of the abundance of the heart that the mouth speaks.
>
> *Luke* 6:45 *(*NRSV*)*

The only way to clean up our language is to have a change of heart!

I close with this reassurance to those who have broken the Third Commandment and misused God's name. Remember—all is not lost. Even if you have not cared much for God's name in the past, even so God still cares for yours. Indeed, in the Bible God says:

> I have written your name on the palms of my hands.
>
> *Isaiah* 49:16 (GN)

He is ready, willing, and able to forgive all the past misuse of His name. He has already accepted you into His heart; He only asks that you accept Him into yours. Welcome His name as your highest and best name!

God's character is flawless. His authority is matchless. And His purpose is to bless. He wants nothing more than for you to experience for yourself the glory and honor of His matchless name. Amen.

Study Guide: God's Last Name Isn't "Damn"!

75 Minutes

Introduction (10 minutes)

Briefly

Have each participant share their first name and what their name means to them. Is it a family name? Is there a story behind their name? What do they like best about their name?

Opening Discussion/Warm Up (5 minutes)

Why is a "good name" a life or death business concern? Why is it a life or death concern for God?

God's Name(5 minutes)

What is the name God gave for Himself? (Genesis 3:13–14)

What does this name mean?

God Is Sensitive about His Name (10 minutes)

According to the story found in Leviticus 24:10–16, is God sensitive about the misuse of His name?

According to Matthew 6:9 is Jesus sensitive about God's name?

What might cause you to be sensitive about the use of your name? Might God feel the same way?

Does a name suggest anything about a person's character and/or authority?

How Do We Misuse God's Name? (10 minutes)

Scripture says:

> You shall not take the name of the Lord thy God in vain.
>
> *Exodus 20:7 (KJV)*

Webster's dictionary defines "vain" as "empty, worthless, and futile." So how is misusing God's name empty, worthless, and futile?

In our current culture in America, there is generally zero tolerance for the "n-word" when referring to African Americans. Why would anyone suppose God to be any more tolerant with the abuse of His name?

The Promise and Blessing of God's Name (5 minutes)

Read out loud the Biblical promises connected to God's name:

> Security— "The *name* of the Lord is a strong tower; the righteous run to it and are safe."
>
> *(Proverbs* 18:10*)*

> Help— "Our help is in the *name* of the Lord."
>
> *(Psalm* 124:8*)*

> Gladness— "...our heart is glad ...because we trust in His holy *name.*"
>
> *(Psalm* 33:21*)*

> Salvation— "Everyone who calls on the *name* of the Lord will be saved."
>
> *(Romans* 10:13*)*

> Promise— "Ask anything, using my *name,* and I will do it."
>
> *(John* 14:14, *Living Bible)*

According to Psalm 61:5, is there a blessing connected with reverence for God's name?

Honoring God's Name (10 minutes)

In the Lord's Prayer, what does "hallowed be thy name" mean?

What does one do to "set apart" God's name?

When you misuse God's name does that misrepresent God to others? Just how seriously does God take this?

What standard does God expect for those who call upon His name?

> Let everyone who nameth the *name* of Christ depart from iniquity.
>
> 2 *Tim.* 2:19 (KJV)

Conclusion (10 minutes)

According to Scripture our words reflect our hearts:

> Out of the abundance of the heart the mouth speaks.
>
> *Luke* 6:45 (NRSV)

Meet one-on-one with a partner and share together how your use of God's name reflects what's in your heart.

Wrap Up (10 minutes)

Share your prayer requests with one another.

Confirm the date and location of the next meeting.

Close by reading out loud the following prayer.

Dear God,

We are entirely too casual when speaking Your holy name! We have used it to curse others. We have misused it in concession to peer pressure and fitting in. Too rarely do we employ Your name to praise You and to bless others! Lord, forgive our abuse, and help us to reverence Your name in all that we do and say. The day is coming when at the sound of your name every knee shall bow and every tongue shall confess You to be Lord. Until that day Lord, help us to tame our tongues. Amen.

Command Four: *If the Devil Can't Make You Bad, He'll Make You Busy!*

The plot to kill Him began on the Sabbath! The Pharisees had suspected for some time that Jesus was a fraud, and at last they had their evidence, for He deliberately broke God's Fourth Commandment, and no heaven-sent messiah would ever violate the Sabbath!

Earlier that same Sabbath day, authorities had caught Jesus's hungry disciples plucking grains of wheat to eat—a scandal in their time—but Jesus Himself had not done it, so He was not accused. But later that same afternoon, in the synagogue of all places, Jesus knowingly healed a man's crippled hand! Before the healing He was reminded it was the Lord's Day. Indeed, He was pointedly asked if it was lawful to heal on the Sabbath. But the question just made Jesus angry. He mumbled something about it "being lawful to do good on the Sabbath" and then turned and told the man, "Stretch out your hand," whereupon Jesus healed it. So, at last, the authorities had their evidence. No heaven-sent messiah would ever violate the Sabbath!

For months the Pharisees had scrutinized Jesus's every move. They watched closely as he healed the sick, cured the lepers, gave sight to the blind, and preached good news to the poor. The miracles were difficult to comprehend, and His preaching was next to impossible to argue against. Indeed, up to that point, Jesus had made a compelling case for being God's man. *But* no messiah would ever violate the Fourth Commandment! It was God's law! This was the turning point. Jesus fell from Messiah to monster in the eyes of the Jewish authorities—when He broke the Sabbath! It was then that the Pharisees plotted to destroy Him!

The Sabbath's Bible Background:

We moderns might not consider the Sabbath a big deal, but the Jews of Jesus's day sure did. They were fanatical about it because they understood it to be the centerpiece of their sacred law and temple culture. It was a day governed by 1,521 laws. The Jews of Jesus's day observed the Sabbath with life and death seriousness. Indeed, during the Maccabean Revolt 160 years before Jesus's time, a company of one thousand Jewish fighters allowed themselves to be hacked to death rather than violate the Sabbath by defending themselves! The Jews took the Sabbath seriously because God took it seriously, and they fully expected that God's anointed messiah would also take it seriously.

In New York, Rio de Janeiro, and Hong Kong, the Sabbath is considered by many an occasion for sipping a latte and reading the Sunday paper. Modern sensibilities find it next to impossible to believe that Jesus's death was fated on a violation of the Sabbath! But for the Jews of Jesus's day, the Sabbath was a lifeline to God, a spiritual anchor, and a principle worth killing and dying for. After all, the Fourth Commandment was crystal clear:

> Remember the Sabbath by keeping it holy!
>
> *Exodus* 20:8

As far as the Jews were concerned, the rhythm of six days of work and one day of rest was as necessary as breathing. Indeed, to break the Sabbath was to stop breathing. God Himself emphasized the life and death nature of the Sabbath with His very own command:

> Everyone who profanes it (Sabbath) shall surely be put to death.
>
> *Exodus* 31:14 *(*NKJV*)*

This was no idle threat. God was fully prepared to execute the letter of this law as noted in Scripture:

> Once, while the Israelites were still in the wilderness, a man was found gathering firewood on the Sabbath. He was taken to Moses, Aaron, and the whole community, and was put under guard, because it was not clear what should be done with him. Then the Lord said to Moses, "The man must be put to death; the whole community is to stone him to death outside the camp." So the whole community took him outside the camp and stoned him to death, as the Lord had commanded."
>
> *Numbers* 15:32–36 *(*GN*)*

Today, readers of the New Testament villainize such zeal. It is presumed that the scribes and Pharisees of Jesus' day were nothing but fanatics. But the Pharisees were not crazy. They correctly understood the Fourth Commandment to be a spiritual mandate from God, and they believed with all their heart and soul that God's blessing depended upon the quality of their Sabbath observance. After all, God had said so through the prophet Isaiah:

> If you watch your step on the Sabbath
> And don't use my holy day for personal advantage,
> If you treat the Sabbath as a day of joy,
> God's holy day as a celebration,
> If you honor it by refusing "business as usual,"

> Making money, running here and there—
> Then you'll be free to enjoy God!
> Oh, I'll make you ride high and soar above it all.
> I'll make you feast...
>
> *Isaiah 58:13–14 (The Message)*

Sabbath observance was a sacred trust from God to the people of Israel, and a necessary condition for God's blessing. It was a positive command that provided rest for both man and beast. The scribes and Pharisees were convinced that the welfare of their nation depended upon a strict observance of this command. The prophet Jeremiah himself gave voice to the fear of what could happen if the Sabbath was not properly honored:

> But if you do not obey me (God), to keep the Sabbath day holy ...then I will kindle an unquenchable fire...
>
> *Jeremiah 17:27*

The Pharisees were not reacting irrationally when Jesus appeared to dismiss the sanctity of the Sabbath. And they weren't alone with their concerns. Even Jesus's own cousin, John the Baptist, openly questioned whether Jesus was the legitimate Messiah because of His unorthodox behavior and seeming uneven observance of God's law.

Of course the New Testament record confirms that Jesus did in fact honor both the letter and the spirit of the Sabbath command. Luke 4:16 confirms:

> ...and on the Sabbath day He (Jesus) went into the synagogue, *as was His custom...*
>
> *Luke* 4:16

Clearly, Jesus observed the Sabbath by attending worship at the local synagogue. Indeed, when reading through the Gospels, Jesus is described as doing the following on the Sabbath:

walking (Matt. 12:1),
worshiping in the synagogue (Matt. 12:9),
sharing meals with friends (Luke 14:1),
visiting invalids (John 5:2–9),
teaching (Luke 4:31),
healing (Luke 13:10–13),
talking and disputing (Luke 14:3ff).

Unfortunately, the Jewish Scribes and Pharisees only knew what their own eyes told them, which was that Jesus seemed to play fast and loose with the Sabbath. They therefore concluded He was a fraud.

It's About Time, and Who Gets It!

God created the Sabbath to be a rest and refreshment for man and beast. In other words, it was intended for our benefit. Jesus said of it:

> The Sabbath was made for man, and not man for the Sabbath.
>
> *Mark* 2:27

Life as God created it was to be a rhythm of labor and leisure, work and worship. It's how the universe was made—six days of creation and one day of rest. It continues to be how the universe works—a rhythm of effort and ease.

And it was not just resting *from* labor, but resting *in* the Lord. It was more than a day to do nothing; it was a day to be in the presence of God! Not only do our bodies tire, but our souls get weary, and they are refreshed in the same way they were made—in the hands of God.

The Sabbath was also a day of divine justice—a day when everyone was equal before God, rich and poor alike. Rest was not reserved only for those who could afford it. It was for every man, woman, and child—free or slave. Indeed, it was for every beast of burden, and even for the land.

The rhythm of the Sabbath was to be a blessing, not a burden. But the Jewish authorities became legalists who threatened forced observance. Because of their zeal for God's law they turned the Sabbath into an obligation. The day set apart for the joy of the Lord had mutated into more lifeless religion. The letter of the law overshadowed its spirit.

But even if this was so, it must be noted that the scribes and Pharisees of Jesus's day were closer to God's intention for the Sabbath than we are today! They, at least, took it seriously. Today, we simply ignore it. Unfortunately our health and well-ing pay a predictable price for neglecting the rhythm of weekly rest. Doctors now dispense massive quantities of sedatives, tranquilizers, nerve pills, antidepressants. Many of these medications attempt to make up for all the rest we've neglected in Sabbaths gone by. The Lord's Day rewards the faithful for doing nothing, but we moderns just can't tolerate doing nothing. We are too busy attending to the tyranny of the urgent …to all the little things of our lives that add up to nothing.

There is an old saying, "If the devil can't make you bad, he'll make you busy." I dare say that most folks today don't see themselves as bad people, but they certainly do see themselves as busy. Indeed, for most people in our culture to be described as "busy" is considered a compliment. But there is such a thing as being too busy. We're too busy when we hurry past the most important things of all: God, family, community, health, new ideas, and fresh visions. Ask yourself, how many people are now unemployed or underemployed because they haven't had a fresh idea in years?

Americans today are too busy. God, family, and community have all taken a back seat to our many pursuits, and the devil couldn't be more delighted. He doesn't have to make you bad to take you down to hell. If you're busy enough, you'll take yourself!

A Balanced Life

The elements of a balanced life are simple. We are to:

- Work at work.
- Play at play.
- And worship at worship.

Too many Americans today have confused these priorities. Instead we:

- Worship work.
- Work at play.
- And play at worship.

The results have been predictable. Fatigue, alienation, and frustration. Anxiety stalks many, devouring those who are not grounded to something deeper. It's not supposed to be this way, and we know it, but we can't seem to break away from the vicious cycle in which we find ourselves. Time won't to allow us.

We've invented a lot of timesaving devices. The introduction of the computer was supposed to give us more free time and save stress. But computers have us working harder than ever because they force a higher standard of precision and images. And this stepped-up demand does not stop with computers. Cell phones were supposed to make life easier, but they have become a ball and chain around our necks. We're always on call, making a day off a joke. We can travel to the distant bounds of the globe, but we are still only one phone number away from the demands of our office. Some of us are more enslaved than ever to the tedium of work, leaving us dazed, confused, and disoriented. For many, their primary relationship is no longer at home but at work. After all, it is at work that we get our personal support, sense of belonging, and where our deepest conversations take place. Our family life has turned into an emotional work out. We drive home from the office contemplating the arguments, the chores, the disconnection, and the various crises that make home life more of a storm than a refuge. Our marriages and children require more work than we bargained for, and many of us feel too overwhelmed to give them the time and attention they require. After all, we give our best at the office, with little left over for the family! Here the devil laughs. Again, he doesn't have to make us bad, just busy.

With such forces at work it is little wonder that Sunday becomes our day for sleep and play. We snooze in to catch up on rest and then lounge with the Sunday paper to prolong that rest. We might take a run to work off some of the extra calories we ingested from all our anxious eating during the week. We then watch sports, because it a great way to escape the emotional demands of the marriage and family …better to watch professional athletes battle than to battle with our spouse and children! Sunday night is family time. We don't actually talk with one another. We just pig out in front of the TV together. Later, before bed, we boot up our computers and cell phones to get a head start on the coming week.

It's got us all exhausted, anxious, and completely disconnected from the things that matter most. We know this, but still the rest and community we want elude us. There never seems to be the time!

So, in a nutshell, the Sabbath is all about time and who we give it to.

A Restful Sabbath

the obvious question is "What does a healthy Sabbath look like?" Clearly, it isn't the fanatical observance that the Pharisees enforced. Neither is it our modern indifference. Here, Jesus's example is instructive. He always attended the local synagogue on the Sabbath. He didn't sleep in, or let poor teaching and bad music keep Him away. He always attended worship. And He Himself did a lot of teaching on the Sabbath. Obviously, He considered God's word essential for rest. Evidently, He knew that real rest was more than doing nothing. It was giving God the opportunity to go to work on us—to minister to our hearts, to refresh our minds, and to renew our souls.

Jesus also spent His Sabbath at the table sharing meals with family, friends, and neighbors—talking, discussing issues, disputing points of theology, etc. He didn't just consume food; He shared the fellowship of a meal! This is a practice that we have all but lost in today's culture. Sitting down at the dinner table so that a meal and some meaningful conversation can be shared.

Permit me a slight digression here.

Have you noticed that the architecture of our homes in America has steadily changed over the past fifty years? The dining rooms have been shrinking while the master bathrooms have been getting bigger. Evidently we are spending more and more time alone in our bathrooms, and less and less time together as a family at meals. Indeed, Americans aren't sitting down together for meals much anymore. During the work week meals are picked up at the fast-food window or distributed individually as family members dribble home—usually in front of the television. A family meal may be all but impossible given our different schedules, but this doesn't make its absence any less destructive.

It is no accident that a shared meal is at the center of both Jewish and Christian worship. For Jews the Sabbath begins each Friday night with a shared meal. For the Christian the Sunday worship climaxes with the celebration of the Lord's Supper. Obviously, there is something sacred in a shared meal. And it is no surprise that for most holidays: Christmas, Easter, Thanksgiving, July 4th picnics, Memorial Day and Labor Day cook-outs, a shared meal is at the center of our celebration.

There are different ways to observe the Sabbath ...but all of them will include a shared meal. To break bread, enjoy stories and laughter, and welcome the Lord's presence is at the very essence of our religion.

Conclusion

The Gospels also tell us of something else that Jesus did on the Sabbath, something that I have yet to mention, something truly remarkable. The Scriptures tell us that on the Sabbath Jesus descended into hell. He was crucified on a Friday morning and died that afternoon at three o'clock, just before the start of the Jewish Sabbath. This means that Jesus spent that particular Sabbath in hell—just as the Apostle's Creed affirms:

> He suffered under Pontius Pilot,
> was crucified, dead, and buried.
> He descended into hell...

Most of the world may be too busy to take time for the Lord, even on the Sabbath. But the good news of the Gospel is that the Lord Himself is never too busy for us—not even on His dying day. Scripture tells us that after His death on the cross Jesus went looking for those who needed Him most—those imprisoned in hell. The Word says:

> ...He went and preached to the spirits in prison who disobeyed long ago...
>
> 1 *Peter* 3:19–20

This is nothing more than what the psalmist had already celebrated.

> If I make my bed in hell, behold, You are there.
>
> *Psalm* 139:8 (NKJV)

That Jesus spent a Sabbath in hell is a mystery that continues to confound tidy theologies. But think of it, if the Lord is willing to spend a Sabbath looking for sinners in hell, then there is no day too sacred and no place too profane that prevents Him for seeking you. Indeed, to this day Jesus still looks for those who need Him most, and He still heals on the Sabbath. Why? Because for reasons only unconditional love can explain, He wants to spend time with you and me, which is what the Sabbath is all about—it's all about time, and who you spend it with! Amen.

Study Guide: If the Devil Can't Make You Bad, He'll Make You Busy!

90 minutes

Introduction (5 minutes)

Have each participant vote with their feet …have them go to one end of the room if Sunday feels like the first day of the week, and to the other end of the room if Sunday seems like the last day of the week. Have both sides explain why.

Opening Discussion/Warm Up (20 minutes)

Read aloud the Fourth Commandment:

> Remember the Sabbath and keep in holy! Six days you shall labor, and do all your work; but the seventh day is a Sabbath to the Lord your God; in it you shall not do any work…
>
> *Exodus* 20:8

In each of the four Gospels Jesus is described as being quite active during the Sabbath (healing, teaching, walking, miracle-working). Read out loud Matthew 12:1–16. You can also look at:

> walking (Matt. 12:1),
> worshiping in the synagogue (Matt. 12:9),
> sharing meals with friends (Luke 14:1),
> visiting invalids (John 5:2–9),
> teaching (Luke 4:31),
> healing (Luke 13:13),
> talking and disputing (Luke 14).

Take a vote—was it reasonable for the Jewish Pharisees to question Jesus's observance of the Fourth Commandment? What about Jesus's behavior on the Sabbath was right or wrong?

The Sabbath's Bible Background (10 minutes)

Assign readers to each of the four passages, and have them read to the group out loud.

> Everyone who profanes it (Sabbath) shall surely be put to death.
>
> *Exodus* 31:14

> Once, while the Israelites were still in the wilderness, a man was found gathering firewood on the Sabbath. He was taken to Moses, Aaron, and the whole community, and was put under guard, because it was not clear what should be done with him. Then the Lord said to Moses, "The man must be put to death; the whole community is to stone him to death outside the camp." So the whole community took him outside the camp and stoned him to death, as the Lord had commanded.
>
> *Numbers* 15:32–36 *(*GN*)*

> If you watch your step on the Sabbath
> And don't use my holy day for personal advantage,
> If you treat the Sabbath as a day of joy,
> God's holy day as a celebration,
> If you honor it by refusing "business as usual,"
> Making money, running here and there—
> Then you'll be free to enjoy God!
> Oh, I'll make you ride high and soar above it all.
> I'll make you feast…
>
> *Isaiah* 58:13–14 *(The Message)*

> But if you do not listen to me, to keep the Sabbath day holy …then I will kindle an unquenchable fire…
>
> *Jeremiah* 17:27

Based on the above passages does God have a clear and firm standard when it comes to observing the Sabbath?

Sabbath: It's about Time, and Who Gets It(20 minutes)

What does the following phrase mean to you? "The Sabbath is not just resting *from* labor, but resting *in* the Lord." In your day-to-day life, what would this actually look like?

What does the following phrase mean? "If the devil can't make you bad, he'll make you busy?" In your day-to-day life is your time under your control? What would you have to do to get more of your time under your control?

A Balanced Life (20 minutes)

Ideally we are to:

Work at work.
Play at play.
Worship during worship.

But today it's been said that we:

Worship work.
Work at play.
Play at worship.

What has happened to make our lives so frantic?

Will you ever "find the time" to do the things God prescribes for health and well-being like a Sabbath, or must you "make the time?"

Go one-on-one with another participant and together make specific plans/action steps for what you will do to secure your Sabbath observance. Note the specific changes you will make, and hold each other accountable for these changes.

A Restful Sabbath (10 Minutes)

Conclude your study by sitting together around a dining room table, sharing a snack, and discussing when and how your respective families share a family meal ...especially on the Sabbath.

Wrap Up(5 minutes)

Share your prayer requests with one another.

Confirm the date and location of the next meeting.

Close by reading out loud the following prayer.

Dear God,

We are busy and distracted with many things. But in the end, Lord, our time with You is what makes the biggest difference. Help us to establish our priorities. May time with You be written first on our calendars rather than trying to squeeze You into the leftovers of our day. And, Lord, help us to set aside a personal Sabbath—a day in which we do more than rest from work. May we take the time to rest in You. Lord, we know Your command; Your prescription is clear. Help us to take time for You, for You never fail to take time for us! Amen.

Interlude:
Jonah: the Prophet Who Learned to Obey!

I have trouble with obedience, and I have a stack of speeding tickets to prove it. I've never responded well to commands, even when they are for my own good. I've insisted on going my own way and doing my own thing. I don't like anyone telling me what I can and cannot do. I just want to be free!

Scripture tells me I'm not alone. Adam and Eve ran into trouble with obedience straight away ...They were given a perfect world with but one command—don't eat the forbidden fruit—and of course they disobeyed. King David also had trouble with obedience. God showered him with power, riches, and blessings uncounted, still it wasn't enough to obey the most obvious restrictions— "Do not commit adultery, do not murder, and do not lie." David disobeyed them all. King Solomon, St. Peter, and St. Paul were all deeply committed to God, but still they struggled with obedience. In fact all God's saints had trouble with obedience, so why should you or I be any different?

The truth is we were born ornery and resistant to any kind of compliance. We sprang from our mothers' wombs with the stubborn belief that the world revolved around us. We didn't acquire this instinct for disobedience while growing up. We were born with it. The Bible is clear that we all are born with disobedience in our hearts. Indeed, the Bible goes so far as to describe us as "rebels."

> ...People have stubborn and rebellious hearts.
>
> *Jeremiah* 5:23

Kids don't need anyone to teach them to lie, cheat, or steal! They do it naturally. They're told not to eat dessert first, but they pitch a fit, test the boundaries, and reach for the cake. Our little darlings don't need to be taught disobedience. They have a Ph.D. in the subject long before nursery school. And it's not something they'll grow out of. At eighty-three years old, they'll still struggle obeying the rules at the retirement home. The bottom line is that all human beings everywhere have a fundamental problem with obedience, because we want to follow our own dictates over anyone else's—God's included!

Recently I visited a huge Christian bookstore in search of a book on the subject of obedience. Not finding anything on the shelves myself, I asked the customer service attendant for help, but they couldn't find anything either. We searched the store's inventory via computer and amazingly enough; there was not one book in the entire store with the word "obedience" in the title! So I decided just to order one over the Internet, but the only credible book I could find was Eugene Peterson's classic *A Long Obedience in the Same Direction* (which I recommend). I was amazed. Evidently, few are interested in learning about obedience. Interesting! Here we have a subject of crucial importance for marriage, career success, parenting, and of course spiritually, and there isn't much available! But obedience has never been a popular subject.

And why is this? Why do we have such antipathy toward obedience? Some say it's because of laws and values that are woefully out of date. People tire of conforming to yesterday's standards. But does this mean that when our laws are updated and in step with the ethos of our times that we will then become obedient? Let's look at an example.

In September of 2000 the United Nations hosted the Millennium Summit, the largest gathering of world leaders ever. Everyone from the President Clinton to the prime minister of Angola were there—160 presidents, kings, and dictators in all. Together they passed two proclamations—just two! The first barred children younger than eighteen from participation in armed conflict. In other words, no child soldiers! The second condemned the use of children for slavery, sex, and pornography. These two resolutions are certainly in keeping with the twenty-first century values. But has this contemporary proclamation been obeyed? Of course not! There are more child soldiers and sex slaves today than ever before. Just because the law is in step with the times does not mean it will be obeyed. We could replace God's Ten Commandments with an internationally agreed upon twenty-first century list of "ten voluntary values," and you and I would still disobey them. Again, we are rebels. This is not a new idea. The Bible has been saying so for thousands of years. The prophet Jeremiah could not have said it more clearly:

> The heart is deceitful above all things,
> and desperately wicked...
>
> *Jeremiah* 17:9 (NKJV)

It's not outdated laws that are the source of our problem with disobedience; it's our hearts. Our hearts are deceitful, rebellious, and self-centered.

Good News

But let me share some good news. It is this: our salvation is not dependent upon our obedience! Nowhere in the Bible does it say that salvation comes at the price of our compliance. The Bible assures us again and again that salvation starts with faith. The Scripture says:

> Believe in the Lord Jesus, and you will be saved.
>
> *Acts* 16:31

Notice what this passage does *not* say. It does not say "obey the Lord Jesus and you will be saved." It says "believe." If heaven were a place reserved for the obedient it would be empty. As the Scripture says:

> ...all have fallen short of the glory of God...
>
> *Romans* 3:23

The Christian faith proclaims that God's blessings are offered to you and me just as we are. We don't have to clean up our act first and become obedient before God extends His grace. God opens up His storehouse of blessing the instant we open our hearts to Him!

The Prophet Who Would Not Obey

The Bible's most dramatic story of disobedience, and God's grace, is that of the prophet Jonah, the man swallowed by the great whale. Here's his story:

God had directed His prophet Jonah to leave Israel and travel to the great Babylonian city of Nineveh where he was to preach repentance to the city's residents. But it turned out that Jonah was a racist and had no intention of offering salvation to a tribe of people he grew up hating. He didn't want to share anything with his enemies, especially God's mercy. So Jonah disobeyed. He booked passage on a ship sailing the opposite direction. God had directed Jonah east to Nineveh, but Jonah, in a fit of rebellion, sailed west.

He hoped he could outrun God, but that was before his ship reached the open water and the perfect storm exploded. Walls of whitecaps slammed into the ship with remorseless fury. The wind and waves tossed the boat like a cork on boiling water. Everyone on board begged mercy as the vessel threatened to break up. But the prophet Jonah knew what was happening. He knew God's finger had stirred the storm. When all hope of surviving evaporated among the crew, Jonah stepped forward with an eerie calm, explained that the storm was God's doing, and that by throwing him overboard they would spare their lives. Reluctantly, the crew did as Jonah directed, and as soon as they threw Jonah into the boiling sea, the storm began to calm.

But for Jonah, the lesson on obedience had just begun, for out of the depths a huge whale stalked him until it opened its mammoth jaws to swallow Jonah whole. There, in the deepest darkness he had ever known, floating in half-digested fish guts and putrid slime, Jonah did what he knew he had to do. He prayed. He called upon the very God he had disobeyed, and begged for mercy. God, of course, had no reason to respond. He was well within his rights to reserve an exquisitely agonizing death inside the whale's digestive juices. But God had every intention of fulfilling His divinely appointed mission through His chosen prophet. For three days Jonah prayed and the great whale swam, until at last, in one heaving wretch, the prophet was thrown up on the shore. There, Jonah again heard God speak, "Get up, go to Nineveh, that great city, and proclaim to it the message that I tell you." This time the prophet obeyed. He made his way to Nineveh, and once there proclaimed God's word, whereupon the whole city believed, repented, and humbled themselves before the Lord! This was the very thing the prophet Jonah had feared—that his mortal enemies the Babylonians would be saved by God's gracious mercy. But not even his direct disobedience could prevent God from fulfilling His errand of mercy.

Like I said, everyone, even God's saints, has trouble with obedience. But it is also true that God can redeem anyone's disobedience into His mercy!

A Surprising Benefit

Here we are left with a major question. For if we can break all the rules and yet still not thwart God's plan or purpose, what is the value of obedience, and why bother with it in the first place? Allow me to answer with an illustration.

I just returned from Haiti. The government there has been in shambles, and obedience to the rule of law is on thin ground. Indeed, there are infinitely more laws and restrictions to obey in the U.S. than there are in Haiti. In Haiti there are no homeowners associations, no detailed building codes on plumbing, no aggressive statutes on tax collection or gun ownership. There are infinitely more laws in the United States than in Haiti, but it's obvious that the people of the United States are far freer. The Haitians may have fewer laws and so fewer demands for obedience, but they are slaves to chaos! And when the great earthquake hit on January 12th, 2010 the country's buildings, constructed without codes as they were, crumbled like graham crackers in the fist of a child.

Obedience and freedom are two sides of the same coin. This, of course, is not what is popularly broadcast today. Freedom is more closely associated with rebellion than responsibility. Americans are used to celebrating their freedom to the tune of Steppenwolf's "Born to Be Wild." But this association defies common sense and our own experience! After all, to which child is a parent going to give more freedom—to the obedient or disobedient child? And to whom will banks lend more freely—those who obey bank procedures or those who don't? And which businesses will customers reward with more business—those that obey product standards or those who don't? Common sense informs us that obedience and freedom are two sides of the same coin.

The spiritual principle here is simple: The more we obey God, the more freedom we enjoy. This is initially counterintuitive, but that's only because we've confused freedom with license. License is to do whatever is wanted. But true freedom is to enjoy the opportunity to do what is best. Freedom isn't doing anything you like. If that were so then drug addicts and anarchists would be counted among the most free, but obviously this isn't so. True freedom means to enjoy the liberty to pursue the best in life.

Let me offer another illustration—this one from nature.

Which dog is happier...the wild dog that runs untamed in the wilderness and does whatever it wants—or the tame dog that obeys a loving master? The wild dog is driven by hunger and fear all day, every day. It does whatever it wants, but the only thing it wants is to do is to eat. It has no master, but neither does it enjoy protection, comfort, and peace. The tame dog, however, doesn't fret for its next meal. He knows he will not only be fed well, but that his needs and comfort will be secured. He trusts his master for what is good, and so he is pleased to obey. The concern of the wild dog is just to stay alive. But the concern of the tame dog is to be the best dog he can be.

It's typical in our culture to see obedience as contrary to freedom. But experience reveals that there is no real freedom in rebellion. This is the paradoxical truth of the Christian gospel—there is a surprising freedom in obedience to God. The Lord doesn't want us fretting every day about just staying alive, which is what life is in Haiti today. He wants us to enjoy a life that is free enough to pursue the best—not just for ourselves but for everyone around us. He wants us to obey Him, not to restrict our behavior, but expand our blessings!

Study Guide: Jonah, the Prophet Who Learned to Obey!

90 minutes

Introduction (10 minutes)

Briefly

Have each participant introduce themselves by name, and have each describe any experience with children. Then have them answer the question "Are children obedient by nature?"

Opening Discussion/Warm Up(10 minutes)

Do people have trouble with rules and regulations, or do they just have trouble with obedience itself?

The Problem (10 minutes)

What does the Bible say about human nature?

> …This people has a stubborn and rebellious heart.
>
> *Jeremiah* 5:23

> The heart is deceitful above all things,
> and desperately wicked…
>
> *Jeremiah* 17:9 (NKJV)

If all laws were updated to be perfectly in step with the prevailing culture, would they be obeyed? In other words, do we disobey because we have trouble with the law, or do we disobey simply because we have trouble with obedience?

Good News (15 minutes)

Is our salvation dependent upon our obedience?

> "*Believe* in the Lord Jesus, and you will be saved."
>
> *Acts* 16:31

Has anyone but Jesus Himself obeyed perfectly?

> ...for *all* have sinned and fallen short of the glory of God.
>
> *Romans* 3:23

Healthy parents don't always love what their children do, but they never stop loving their children. Is such unconditional love a glimmer of God's love for us?

The Prophet Who Would Not Obey! (30 *minutes*)

Read together chapter one of Jonah. What did God order Jonah to do? Did he obey? Why?

Was Jonah completely free to do what he wanted?

How yes?

How no?

According to Jonah 4:1–3 did Jonah feel good about obeying when God gave him a second chance? Does obedience have to be accompanied by good feelings and/or personal agreement?

Surprising Benefit(10 *minutes*)

If we can break all God's rules and yet still not thwart God's mercy, why should we even bother with obedience? Is there any value to it?

Who is freer, the one who breaks all the rules and suffers the consequences, or the one who enjoys the benefits of obedience?

Where would you rather live—vote with your feet. If you would prefer to live in Haiti where there are far fewer laws to obey go to one side of the room. But if you would prefer to live in the litigious United States go to the other side of the room. Explain your answer in terms of freedom (not poverty).

Wrap Up (5 minutes)

Share your prayer requests with one another.

Confirm the date and location of the next meeting.

Close by reading out loud the following prayer:

Dear God,

We have enough experience to know that we are by nature rebels. We insist on going our own way, doing our own thing. Forgive us of our stiff-necked, hard-headed ways. Help us to accept Your life! You promise freedom from selfishness, egotism, and sin. In You we are also released to a life that rises above our own petty concerns. Your Spirit liberates us from a "me-centered life" to a "we-centered life." Lord, into Your hands we commend our spirits, and pray that in all things we would have the faith to obey You in all things. Amen.

Command Five:
Don't Dump on Dad!

Recently I received a letter from a dedicated man who had served our country in war and peace all over the world in the armed forces. His letter was notable because it forwarded a painful e-mail his eighteen-year-old son sent him. In it his son skewered him for being a lousy parent. Here is what the son wrote:

> Dad!
>
> You have one kid, that's it! After me there is no more. What is so much more important than seeing your son play his senior year of high school basketball? If you don't go to all of my games, I am going to be pissed off and promise to remember it for the rest of my life. You are my parent. I am your kid. This is my last year with you, so don't be a dick and not show up. You are the only parent who misses big tournaments. If you can't suck it up to support your only son, you shouldn't even have a kid and should be embarrassed to call yourself a father. If you don't put in the effort to at least attend my last tournament in high school, don't expect me to talk about how great you are to anyone. Be a f___ing parent for once! Being a parent isn't just paying for stuff; it's being at stuff that's important to your kid. Don't give me the BS that "you're too busy

or tired." I won't accept that. I won't accept any of your excuses this time, Dad. You are going to the tournament, and you are going to be there the whole time. I am sick and tired of your BS!

Sincerely,
Your Son John

Wow! I'd say the young man dumped all over his dad. I'm familiar with the family's circumstances. The father is a single parent. His wife died tragically. He has served with distinction as a commander in the U.S. Navy. He even served in the infamous "Green Zone" of Bagdad during the most dangerous period of the war in Iraq. He's a recovering alcoholic. His life has not been the easiest. But the son's letter has zero empathy for his father. It's an angry rant from an angry young man. Certainly the boy has reasons to be upset: He lost his mother. His father could not give him the time and attention he needed. He is anxious for his future. But this does not give him license to dump all over his dad. It's a classic case of a child being wounded by a well-intentioned parent. All of which brings us to the Fifth Commandment, which is:

> Honor your father and your mother...
>
> *Exodus* 20:12

The Fifth Commandment

Before addressing the specifics of the Fifth Commandment, let me first offer a broad overview.

The Ten Commandments can be divided into two basic themes. The first four address our vertical relationship with God.

> Commandment #1—Worship only God
>
> Commandment #2—No idols for God

Commandment #3—Honor God's name
Commandment #4—Honor God's day

Again, the focus of the first four commandments is God and how to relate to Him. The last six commandments address our horizontal relationship with other people:

Commandment #5—Honor your parents
Commandment #6—Don't murder
Commandment #7—No adultery
Commandment #8—Don't steal
Commandment #9—Don't lie
Commandment #10—Don't envy

In essence, commandments five through ten are all about human relationships. Indeed, they form the basis for civil society; they are the building blocks for all human interaction. It's notable how God begins them—not as one might expect. God doesn't begin with marriage and how husbands and wives should treat each other. Neither does God start with how parents should treat their children. Instead, God starts with children and how they are to honor their parents! Indeed, the elemental importance of honoring parents is a recurring theme throughout scripture. The Old Testament says:

> Cursed is the man who dishonors his father or his mother…
>
> *Deuteronomy* 27:16

The New Testament does not relax the standard. It says,

> Children, obey your parents in everything, for this pleases the Lord.
>
> *Colossians* 3:20

Other religions agree with this principle of honoring one's parents. For example, in Buddhism we find:

> Those who wish to be born in the Pure Land of Buddha ...should act filially towards their parents and support them.
>
> *Meditation on Buddha Amitayus*, 27

In Islam the Koran says:

> Thy Lord has decreed... that you be kind to parents... address them in terms of honor.
>
> *Qur'an* 17.23

Evidently, the principle of honoring parents is all but universal.

Why Is This Commandment So Important?

So why doesn't God begin His laws for human interaction and civility with something like, "Honor thy spouse?" or "Love your neighbor as yourself." Why is honoring parents so essential to any civilized society? The answer is because the parent-child relationship is a foundation for all relationships. We may dream of a satisfying marriage, of having fun with our own kids, and of being popular and successful at work, but if we grow up without first honoring our parents then the Scriptures caution that our relational foundation is faulty. Without first learning to honor our parents we are not likely as adults to honor our spouse, children, boss, friend; and most fundamental of all, we aren't likely to honor God! Simply put, the parent-child relationship casts the longest relational shadow.

But why does the commandment focus on "honor" instead of love? Isn't love more important? Yes. But parents can forfeit their children's love through abuse, neglect, and indifference. Frankly, some parents are not worthy of their children's love.

I recently read a horrible news story that took place in my birthplace of Harrisburg, Pennsylvania; the story involved a father and mother convicted of the third-degree murder in the tragic death of their handicapped ten-year-old daughter. The girl had cerebral palsy, was blind, and was confined to a wheel chair. Her mother accidently placed her in a bathtub full of scalding water, that burned the girl with third-degree wounds over one-third of her body. This was a terrible mistake on the mother's part but certainly not criminal. The crime came later. The parents did not get their daughter to medical care. The husband worked two jobs, but didn't have any medical insurance. It was an expense they couldn't afford. What's more, the thought of waiting endless hours at a hospital emergency room seemed impossible—the father assumed he couldn't take the time off from work. In the mean time the girl's burns got infected, and for eight days she suffered searing pain. The parents did not notify anyone until after they found their daughter dead in her bed.

What a horror story! Certainly these two parents did not merit the love of their daughter. And your own parents may not have merited your love. Your parents may have been abusive, alcoholics, molesters, uninterested, or just plain incompetent. But keep in mind that Commandment Five does not demand love. It does not insist that you have warm and fuzzy feelings for your parents. It simply states, "*Honor* your father and your mother."

Here, an important principle is at stake. It is this. The "office" of parent transcends the merits or failures of any individual parent. Your father and mother may have been monsters and unworthy, but that still does not excuse you from honoring their place in your life. Why? Because for better or worse you came from your parents, so at a minimum you owe them consideration for giving you life. After all, they did not abort you. They endured the ordeals of pregnancy and birth. They fed you and changed your diapers. As parents they may have done a lot wrong, but they got one thing right—they brought you into the world, and as a consequence your life is inescapably connected with theirs. You may not like them, trust them, or want anything to do with them. Fine. But to think that you can escape their influence is an illusion. Remember, President Obama did not grow up with his father at home. Indeed, he grew up Hawaii and Indonesia while his father lived half a world away in Kenya, East Africa. Even so, the president himself acknowledges his father's influence. For better or worse, the shadow of parents occupies a major place, and the Bible's wisdom directs you to honor their place.

There is another important consideration. By honoring your parents (regardless of their merits) you develop a more realistic worldview—an accurate perspective of your place in the real world. After all, from time to time you will have to deal with disagreeable and dishonorable people who are in authority over you—who are in a position to command respectful compliance. If you're unwilling to at least be considerate of their authority, you're going to have trouble. To think the world revolves around you is a delusion. The Fifth Commandment directs that you honor your father and mother regardless of how good or bad they are, or how you might feel about them. After all, in the real world there will be circumstances that transcend your own feelings.

The perspective that we are not the center of our own universe is formed at an early age, primarily through a child's interaction with parents. I saw a perfect display not long ago in the checkout line at the grocery store.

In front of me was a young mother with two children, one of whom was screaming his head off because his mother wouldn't buy him a plastic pumpkin for Halloween. I was impressed with the mother. She did exactly the right thing …she empathized with the way her son felt, but she also stood her ground. She said, "I'm sorry you feel so bad, Son, but you just can't have it." It was excellent parenting on her part. She didn't waste energy trying to make him feel better, nor did she ignore his desire. She empathized with how he felt but patiently explained herself and stood her ground. Her son was despondent. He wasn't getting what he wanted. But he was getting a more valuable lesson …he was learning that the world didn't revolve around him!

To honor parents is to live out the principle that you are not the center of the universe!

What Does the Commandment Actually Say?

The key word of the Fifth Commandment is of course "honor." Just what does it mean to honor parents? Let's start with what it does *not* mean.

First, Commandment Five does not demand love and affection for parents! The command says "honor" not love. In fact, I cannot think of a single verse in the Bible that commands children to "love" their parents. Neither does it insist that you admire your parents. Some parents can be an inspiration—the very example of the scripture that says:

> Parents are the pride of their children.
>
> *Proverbs* 17:6

But some parents are not worthy of admiration. Remember the movie *Forrest Gump?* Forrest's childhood girl friend Jennie had a sexually abusive and violent father. His memory haunted her, and all but ruined her adult life. Such a father was not worthy of admiration.

Finally, Commandment Five does not demand that you always obey parents. Some abusive parents cannot be obeyed—like Jennie's father in *Forrest Gump.* It is true that the New Testament says,

> Children, obey your parents in the Lord…
>
> *Ephesians* 6:1

But note how this particular passage ends. "Children, obey your parents *in the Lord.*" Parents are to be obeyed as they are "in the Lord"—within God's will and word. God does not want children submitting themselves to some abusive situation. Honoring parents does not mean that children are to blindly submit to anything a parent demands! You are to obey parents as long as they themselves are obedient to God.

Some mothers or fathers can be cruel, indifferent, and even twisted. The idea of honoring them may seem unimaginable. But Commandment Five is not conditional. It does not say, "If you had a good experience growing up with your parents—honor them." No, it says simply "honor you mother and father." This puts some individuals in a very tough position, but there is an answer. The answer has to do with the exact meaning of the word "honor."

The word "honor" literally means "to give weight to." In other words, you are not to take parents lightly. The book of Leviticus expresses it this way.

> Each of you must respect his mother and father.
>
> *Leviticus* 19:3

Said simply, you are to take your parents with the utmost seriousness. This doesn't mean that you must love them, like them, or always obey them. It simply means that you are to take them seriously—you are to show them respect, not because they deserve it, or because you want to give it, but because the "office" of parent requires it.

Why Are We to Honor Our Parents?

The big question is "Why?" Why should you give your parents any more weight than anyone else, especially if they were cruel or indifferent? Here's why. Even if we can't respect parents as individuals, still we are to respect their "office." Let me illustrate what I'm talking about.

If you were subpoenaed to the county courthouse to stand trial, you would address the judge as "Your Honor." It's possible the judge may not be worthy such respect. Indeed, he/she might be a thief, a liar, a cheat, and a drunkard, but nonetheless you would address the judge as "You Honor." Why? Out of respect for their office! This principle is what Commandment Five is all about. Parents are honored whether they are worthy or not because the office of parent is the most important office in civilized society. God created the family as the foundation for human culture, and He created it with certain principles, one of which is that respect for any and all authority begins with the respect for the parent. If a child respects the parent's office he or she is likely to respect the office of teachers, principals, policemen, employers, and above all God. It's just the way our human psychology works.

Here there is a principle, a pattern, and a promise.

To honor fathers and mothers is how we learn at an early age to respect authority. This is the principle behind honoring parents. Martin Luther put it this way, "All authority flows and is propagated from the authority of parents."[3]

There is also a *pattern.* Honoring parents establishes the foundation for all other relationships. The way parents are honored impacts all other intimate relationships. For example, have you noticed that men tend to treat their wives the way they treat their mothers? And isn't it amazing how women tend to marry men like their fathers. Parents are the first intimate relationship, and so that relationship casts the longest shadow.

Finally, there is also a *promise.* The Scripture says,

> Honor you father and mother, *that your days may be long…*
>
> *Exodus* 20:12

This promise is not a guarantee of a ripe old age for those who honor their parents. But the best prescription for a long life is a healthy home, and a healthy relationship with your parents will lay the foundation for your own happy home. Health begets health, and strife begets strife. When you grow up in a family of peace, where order and authority are respected, you are likely to beget peace, health, and a long and fruitful life.

How Do You Make Peace with Your Parents?

So how do you make peace with your parents? How do you honor them if they have brought you pain or abuse?

The first step is to *accept* them. The Scripture says:

> Accept one another …just as Christ accepted you.
>
> *Romans* 15:7

God can use horrible and tragic experiences with parents to accomplish His mysterious purposes. You are neither to ignore nor deny the mistakes of your parents. Instead, you can accept them, trusting that God can and will use them for a greater purpose. As the Scripture promises:

> …*in all things* God works for the good of those who love Him, who have been called according to His purpose.
>
> *Romans* 8:28

"All things" includes the molestation, cruelty, and indifference of parents. God takes what is broken and somehow makes it whole. He transforms pain into power. He redeems our worst into His best. But first we must accept our parents for who they are—sinners, who like us, need God.

The second step is to *forgive.* Modern psychology has made it easy to play the blame game and accuse parents. But as long as you continue to blame parents, nothing gets resolved. As long as you say things like "I'll never do to my children what my parents did to me," then you are still reacting to your parents, which means they are still in control. You are finally free of your parents when you finally forgive them.

A third step to make peace is to *affirm* them. There is great power in affirmation. We all need it, kids and parents alike. Any moron can be negative and criticize. But the Scripture says:

> Whatever is true, whatever is honorable, whatever is just, whatever is pure, whatever is lovely, whatever is gracious, if there is any excellence, if there is anything worthy of praise, think about these things…
>
> *Philippians* 4:8 *(*RSV*)*

Look to the good and affirm it, rather than focusing on the negative and harping on it. Children aren't likely to change long established patterns in their parents. That is God's work. You can, however, affirm the good that you appreciate in your parents. Too many wait until it is too late to affirm parents. Too often it's not until their parents' funerals that appreciation and respect are expressed. There are lots of simple ways to express appreciation: phone calls, a handwritten note, flowers, and a day spent just with them.

And there is one group of parents that deserve a special honor and affirmation, and that is single parents—who either by divorce, separation, or death are forced to lead the family by themselves.

Finally, you are not to *abandon* parents. The Bible is clear that parents are not to be abandoned in their old age. As they get older the roles of responsibility reverse. Growing up they cared for you, but as they grow old you secure them. Commandment Five cares nothing for convenience or ease. You are to honor your parents no matter how inconvenient it may be. There were plenty of times when your parents were inconvenienced when raising you. As they get older, you are called to deal with the inconveniences of their circumstances. The Bible says,

> Children and grandchildren ...should learn first to carry out their religious duties toward their own family and in this way repay their parents and grandparents because this is what pleases God.
>
> 1 *Timothy* 5:4 *(Good News)*

Conclusion:

I started this chapter with a disrespectful e-mail from an angry young man to his father. Even if it was over the top and out of line, still there was good news in it. Clearly the young man was trying to reach out to his dad. He expressed his need for his father's time and attention. In an odd way, it was the ultimate compliment, for his e-mail communicated the desire for his father's love. Obviously, the heart of the son was still connected to the heart of the father, which gives father and son a lot to work with.

But to dump all over his dad as he did is evidence that he will likely disrespect others in the future—college professors, bosses, fathers-in-law, and representatives from the IRS. I know this young man, and I can testify that he has huge potential. But brains, good looks, athleticism, and charm are not enough to make a success of one's life, because life isn't just about ourselves. The world does not revolve around any one person, no matter how much natural talent and personal gifts they may possess. We are not islands unto ourselves. Life is all about the quality of our relationships. If we grow up disrespecting our parents, we are not likely to thrive in the relationships that count the most: our marriages, our children, our friends, our colleagues, and our community.

The principle of God's Fifth Commandment is simple and profound. Those who honor their parents are more than likely to honor their wives and husbands, friends and colleagues, community and government. All relationships spring out of the foundation we establish with our parents, which is exactly why God directs us to honor our father and mother.

Study Guide: Don't Dump on Dad!

90 minutes

Introduction (10 minutes)

Briefly

Have each participant name their favorite parental television character. What is it about this character that makes them your favorite TV mom or dad?

Opening Discussion/Warm Up (15 minutes)

Read the following letter (out loud) from an eighteen-year-old son to his dad. What would you do as a parent if you received this letter from your son? More importantly, *what would you hope to achieve by taking your course of action?*

> Dad!
>
> You have one kid, that's it! After me there is no more. What is so much more important than seeing your son play his senior year of high school basketball? If you don't go to all of my games, I am going to be pissed off and promise to remember it for the rest of my life. You are my parent. I am your kid. This is my last year with you, so don't be a dick and not show up. You are the only parent who misses big tournaments. If you can't suck it up to support your only son, you shouldn't even have a kid and should be embarrassed to call yourself a father. If you don't put in the effort to at least attend my last tournament in high school, don't expect me to talk about how great you are to anyone. Be a f___ing parent for once! Being a parent isn't just paying for stuff; it's being at stuff that's important to your kid. Don't give me the BS that "you're too busy or tired." I won't accept that. I won't accept any of your excuses this time, Dad. You are going to the tournament,

and you are going to be there the whole time. I am sick and tired of your BS!

Overview and Context(10 *minutes)*

The Ten Commandments can be divided into two sections.

Our Relationship with God:

Commandment #1—Worship only God

Commandment #2—No idols

Commandment #3—Honor God's name

Commandment #4—Honor the God's day (Sabbath)

Our Relationship with Others:

Commandment #5—Honor parents

Commandment #6—Don't murder

Commandment #7—No adultery

Commandment #8—Don't steal

Commandment #9—Don't lie

Commandment #10—Don't envy

Of the six commandments dedicated to human relationships, why would God start with children and honoring parents? Why wouldn't God start with "love your neighbor as yourself" or "husbands love your wives, wives respect your husbands"?

How universal among the world's religions is this principle of honoring parents?

In American culture today where is the emphasis? Is it on children honoring their parents, or is it on parents doing all they can for their children? What is driving this emphasis?

Why is this Commandment so important? (15 minutes)

Divide your room into three sections. In one section of the room, gather those who believe that the parent-child relationship is the most influential of all relationships. Have those who think the marital relationship is the most influential in another section. Have those who think some other relationship is the most influential gather in the third section. Discuss within each group the most compelling evidence for your answer. Share your evidence with the larger group.

Reassemble the whole group and share with one another what is right and what is wrong about the statement "The child-parent relationship casts the longest shadow in one's life."

Do you buy the argument that a child who does not learn to "honor" his/her parents is not likely as an adult to respect the authority of others (teachers, coaches, spouses, in-laws, police, etc.)? Share examples.

What does the Fifth Commandment actually say? (15 minutes)

Does the Fifth Commandment demand that we love, admire, or obey parents?

The word "honor" is translated as "to give weight to." Divide into groups of two and come up with different ways a child can respect ("give weight to") a parent who does not merit their love, admiration, or obedience? Share your answers with the larger group.

Why are we to honor our parents? (15 minutes)

Discuss this hypothetical question. If you were to stand trial for some criminal offense, and you knew the presiding judge to be a drunk, a cheat, and a scoundrel, would you still address him/her as "your honor"? Why?

Do you believe that the family is humankind's first and most essential institution? If so, is the "office" of parent the most important office in civilized society? And does this "office" deserve respect regardless of whether the individual parent occupying that office is worthy?

Making peace with parents. (10 *minutes)*

The Scripture says:

> Accept one another . . . just as Christ accepted you.
>
> *Romans* 15:7

Have you accepted your parents as they are, or are you still trying to change them?

Do you believe that God can use even the worst of our experiences with our parents to bring about His best for your lives? Read together:

> . . . *in all things* God works for the good of those who love Him, who have been called according to His purpose.
>
> *Romans* 8:28

Discuss together what is included when the Scripture says "in all things."

If you never forgive your parents, will you ever be free of them, or will you still be negatively influenced by them?

Wrap Up (5 *minutes)*

Share your prayer requests with one another.

Confirm the date and location of the next meeting.

Close by reading out loud the following prayer.

Dear God,

Thank You for this time together. We acknowledge that we are not all equal in life experience. Some of us enjoyed excellent parents, and some endured monsters. We trust You, Lord, to work out Your purposes with both the good and the bad. For those of us who enjoyed terrific parents, we're mindful that we did nothing to deserve them—they are an instance of Your grace in our lives, and we're grateful. And for those of us who endured horrible parents, we too are mindful that we did nothing to deserve them. We also trust that You can transform even horror into healing and holiness.

Lord, help us to accept our parents as they are—broken men and women who need You every bit as much as we do. And help us to go the step further to forgive them. Their wrongs are never right, yet still we can release them from our bitterness, and in so doing we can release ourselves from their influence.

Lord, we ask that You Yourself serve as the perfect parent we never had… as the One who can heal every hurt, salve every sorrow. Amen.

Command Six:

He Murdered His Mother!

I sat dumbfounded! I mean, it just wasn't possible! There I was in Memphis, enjoying a scrumptious Southern fried lunch with old friends at the Blue Plate Café, when suddenly the conversation turned to whispers as I was told about our mutual friend John Brunner and how he strangled his eighty-two-year-old mother! I couldn't take it in. After all, we had all attended the same adult Sunday school class together. John was a good guy—an accountant for the University of Memphis. He was last person anyone could imagine convicted of murdering his mother! Here's the story.

John lived in a small guesthouse behind his mother's property. On the afternoon of July 23, 2006, the two got into an argument after John had expressed concern that she was overmedicating herself. Their exchanged became heated. The intensity escalated. Finally, John's mother lost all composure and started lashing him with her cane. John tried leaving for his car, but his mother followed closely behind flogging him. His patience spent, John whirled around to jerk away her cane, but she grabbed him, they struggled and fell. John landed atop her with his wrist across her throat. She continued to hit him, whereupon he applied pressure with his wrist ...'til she stopped.

What was John thinking?! And how did they ever get into such an absurd circumstance?! During his trial he simply said that he "snapped."

After his mother stopped struggling, John got up then knelt to feel for her pulse, but she was gone. Now John is in federal prison for murder. Never in a million years could anyone have predicted this fate. He was a university accountant for heaven's sake, who attended church every Sunday and who considered himself a "family man." But now he's locked away for the rest of his life for breaking the most obvious command of all.

> Thou shalt not kill.
>
> *Exodus* 20:13 (KJV)

Crazy as John Brunner's story sounds, it's not all that unusual. In a typical year here in the U.S., there are over 20,000 murders and thousands more attempted murders. Most are not premeditated or cold blooded. Most are thoughtless acts of passion. Rare is the person who gets out of bed in the morning knowing they will kill someone. The vast majority of killings are committed by men and women who wake up assuming it's just another day. But then something crazy happens that leads them to a split second choice to kill someone. Justice statistics reveal that only 14 percent of the murders in America involve confirmed strangers. Indeed, most murders (55 percent) are committed by the victim's family members, "friends," or acquaintances. Obviously, when blood runs hot, cold-blooded murder can follow! Oscar Wilde expressed just this idea in his poem "The Ballad of Reading Gaol." He wrote it while himself a prisoner and after having witnessed the execution of a man who had murdered his wife.

Yet each man kills the thing he loves
By each let this be heard
Some do it with a bitter look,
Some with a flattering word,
The coward does it with a kiss,
The brave man with a sword!
Some kill their love when they are young,
And some when they are old;
Some strangle with the hands of Lust
Some with the hands of Gold:
The kindest use a knife, because
The dead so soon grow cold.

Scripture confirms that humanity's very first murder was a hot-blooded family affair. Adam and Eve had two sons. Cain, the eldest, was a farmer. His younger brother Abel was a shepherd. As adults Abel was the more generous and trusting of the two, and God blessed him for it, which provoked envy in Cain. He invited Abel to his farm where in a jealous rage he murdered Abel. He hid the body, but the blood of Abel cried out to God. Keep in mind that this murder occurred *before* God had established any formal law against killing, so Cain's murder didn't technically break any written code. Nonetheless, there was something in the blood that demanded divine justice.

The same remains true today! Innocent blood cries out for divine justice.

Life Is Sacred!

The Sixth Commandment proclaims life to be sacred. Each and every individual is precious because the breath of life is a gift from God, and so is sacred. Our lives are not valued because of our power, position, or possessions. Our lives alone are precious because they are a reflection of God. Genesis 9:6 provides chapter and verse for what I'm saying:

> Whoever sheds the blood of man, by man shall his blood be shed; *for in the image of God has God made man.*
>
> *Genesis* 9:6

God does not distinguish between the life of the good or the bad. The Sixth Commandment isn't concerned for the quality of a life. Life itself is precious. We are all made in the image of God, and this fact alone elevates the value of our lives to being priceless. The Scripture says as much directly:

> ...the payment for a human life is too great. What we could pay would never be enough.
>
> *Psalm* 49:8 *(*GN*)*

Killing another human being, therefore, defaces the image of God. Therefore, an assault upon man is an assault upon God.

What the Law Does Not Say

Here it's instructive to review just what the Sixth Commandment does *not* say. The Sixth Commandment is not a prohibition against all killing. The word "kill" in the sixth commandment is more precisely translated "murder." This understanding is confirmed by what God says in Exodus shortly after He gives His Ten Commandments.

> ...if a man schemes and kills another man deliberately, take him away from my altar and put him to death...
>
> *Exodus* 21:14

The Sixth Commandment is not intended to be a prohibition against hunting animals, war, or capital punishment. Indeed, the Bible describes principles for war in Deuteronomy 20, as well as rules for executing a murderer in Exodus 21. It's reasonable to presume that if the Bible gives rules for war and capital punishment then God is obviously not prohibiting them with the Sixth Commandment. Nonetheless, the command is clearly a prohibition against the kind of murder my friend John Brunner committed against his mother! Regardless of whether or not John got out of bed on July 23, 2006, intending to kill his mother is of no consequence. At some point he made the choice to kill.

Five Modern Applications

You probably don't fuss much about the Sixth Commandment. In twenty-first century America, we tend to presume we've progressed beyond murder. I'm positive John Brunner never gave the Sixth Commandment as much as a passing thought before his mother's death. The standard is obvious. But even the calmest and most reasonable of people can suddenly erupt into murderous rage when provoked. Remember what Ruth Bell Graham, Rev. Billy Graham's wife, said when asked about whether she had ever contemplated divorce? She answered, "Murder yes, divorce no." Given the perfect storm of emotion and circumstance … anyone can be driven over the edge to kill.

What's more, how many have killed their marriage with unchecked rage, strangled their family life with overwork, or mortally wounded the reputation of a colleague with gossip? Some murders are subtle, barely noticeable, but they take life just the same. After all, it's not necessary to pull a gun to take a life. Husbands and wives drain the life out of each other all the time with cruel rage or cold indifference.

And even if your life is in order with a healthy family life, good friends, and fulfilling career, you're still not off the hook when it comes to the Sixth Commandment, for there are five specific issues involving the Sixth Command that vex us all. They are:

1. abortion
2. suicide

3. mercy killing
4. capital punishment
5. war.

Each one involves the premeditated taking of human life. Some, like abortion, are hotly debated and divisive. Others are left in the background of the social debate. But they all involve our collective sanction for taking life. Let's take a brief look at each one in light of the Sixth Commandment.

Abortion

Abortion is of course a hot button issue. It is estimated that since the landmark Roe vs. Wade decision in 1973 over forty million abortions have been performed! Jennifer O'Neill, in her book *You're Not Alone,* claims that 43 percent of all U.S. women who have reached the age of forty-five have had an abortion! She goes on to say that abortion is the number-one medical procedure performed on women in the U.S. today. But I don't know anyone, pro-choice or pro-life, who does not view abortion as a tragedy. The most strident supporter of abortion rights is not happy with our demand for them.

The pro and con arguments don't need to be rehearsed in detail. They boil down to the status given the unborn. Are the unborn subhuman, potentially human, or fully human? If the unborn are subhuman then abortion is an obvious possible choice. If the unborn are potentially human, there will be trouble deciding, but in the end pragmatic considerations will prevail. If, however, the unborn are fully human, then the logic of giving the unborn full legal protection is compelling. Currently U.S. law does not give the unborn full legal recognition ("The unborn have never been recognized in the law as persons in the whole sense," Justice Harry A Blackburn for the Court, *Roe v. Wade*).

Abortion is not a new ethical concern; it was well known in the ancient world. Indeed, the first complete written code of law, the ancient Babylonian Hammurabie Code (1900 BC) enshrined a principle of "the strong should not harm the weak." The code specifically penalized abortions (articles 209 & 210). The ancient Greeks were generally tolerant of abortion, and yet their own Hippocratic Oath (400 BC) specifically condemns it for physicians— "I will not give a woman a remedy to produce abortion."

As for what the Bible itself says about abortion ...very little directly. Still, most Catholics, Protestants, and Pentecostals understand scripture to be prejudiced toward life, with the Sixth Commandment serving as the foundation for that belief. But frankly, the Bible offers no plainly worded, direct prohibition against abortion. The biblical text that can be most directly applied is:

> If some men are fighting and hurt a pregnant woman so that she loses her child, but she is not injured in any other way, the one who hurt her is to be fined whatever amount the woman's husband demands; subject to the approval of the judges. But if the woman herself is injured, the punishment shall be life for life...
>
> *Exodus* 21:22–23 *(*GN*)*

Both sides of the abortion debate use this scripture as a primary proof text for their convictions. The pro-life movement notes that the passage clearly demonstrates how God values the life of the unborn ...that any man who induces a miscarriage or abortion is to be punished. But the pro-choice movement highlights how the passage does not afford the unborn the same status as the mother, and how the event is treated more like a property dispute than a killing.

Most folks of differing opinions aren't convinced with Bible verses. Frankly, scripture doesn't influence what we believe as much as what we believe influences how we interpret scripture.

Research shows that people make their fundamental value decisions based on how they feel more than on what they think or believe. Ultimately, decisions are made in the heart, not by any finely crafted textual/legal arguments. What is persuasive is what is in the heart, and in the end, hearts are changed only with a personal touch from God. Even so, believers are always challenged to reconcile what they feel with God's command: "thou shalt not kill."

Suicide

Suicide is now the second largest killer of American teens. Make no mistake about it, suicide is murder. It is when we murder ourselves, and the Christian church has always preached against it. Indeed, the earliest church would not perform the funerals of those who committed suicide, for they believed that it was the ultimate statement of faithlessness, expressing a hopelessness that denied the power of God to help.

Suicide is no stranger to the Bible. I can think of seven individuals who committed suicide in scripture: Judas, Sampson, King Saul, Saul's armor bearer, Abimelech, Ahithophel, and Zimri. There were also two attempted suicides: Jonah and the Philippian jailer. Each instance was an act of hopeless despair.

I for one don't believe that all who commit suicide are damned. Some individuals suffer serious mental and emotional problems brought on by chemical imbalances and by traumatic experiences. To say that all such people are damned is to unnecessarily limit the reach of God. But make no mistake about it; the Word of God is strident against anyone who would take a life, even if it is their own.

> Don't you know that you yourselves are God's temple and that God's Spirit lives in you? If anyone destroys God's temple, God will destroy him; for God's temple is sacred, and you are that temple.
>
> 1 *Corinthians* 3:16–17

Capital Punishment

Capital punishment is an issue many have trouble with, but the Bible doesn't seem to. The Scripture offers clear provision for capital punishment. For example:

> Anyone who strikes a man and kills him shall surely be put to death.
>
> *Exodus* 21:12

But as clear as the Old Testament is on capital punishment, Jesus Himself did not adhere to its strict standard, taking a more nuanced approach. When asked to decide a case involving capital punishment, that of the woman caught in adultery, Jesus rejected a strict judgment. Instead, He adjudicated a justice that transcended the letter of the law in favor of its spirit, "Let he who is without sin cast the first stone."

The principle problem with capital punishment today is not so much what the Word of God says, but how it is carried out. Statistics reveal that our judicial system does not sentence offenders equally. If you are an African American, you stand a much better chance of being condemned to die in our judicial system than if you are an Anglo American. This is wrong and it is sin. It is a betrayal of the very justice that we profess to uphold. If capital punishment is performed in America, it must be done with a justice or not done at all.

Additionally, we need to acknowledge that our nation's laws on capital punishment are driven more by politics than by any legal or spiritual principle. Politicians in an election year make pronouncements about "getting tough on criminals," and how certain crimes need to be prosecuted to "the fullest extent of the law." Such appeals pander for votes, not justice. Believers are to remember that the Lord came to earth to "seek and to save the lost." His mission was not to make a good man better but a bad man redeemed. That mission is not always best served by killing those who need God's help most.

Mercy Killing

Mercy killing (euthanasia) is ending the life of a person suffering from a terminal illness or incurable disease. The Netherlands was the first country to legalize it in 2002. In the U.S., Oregon enacted a law to allow physician assisted suicide in November of 1994.

Again, the Bible provides a clear standard.

> Many are the afflictions of the righteous, but the Lord delivereth him out of them all.
>
> *Psalm* 34:19 *(*KJV*)*

God gives life, and only God is to take it. We are not to play God. This surely means more pain and suffering for the terminally ill, but the Bible is clear that humanity's biggest enemy is not pain, but the temptation to play God.

Still modern medicine has extended the boundaries of life to the degree that many are no longer able to endure the pain. Do we withhold pain-killing drugs from those in agony to avoid risking their death? Does the principle of life always trump the principle of compassion? Clearly, the Bible has more reverence for life than it has fear of pain.

War

The fifth issue is the biggest—war. Multiple volumes have been written on "just war" theory. According to Catholic theory, two conditions must be present for war to be "just"—there must be the right to go to war (jus ad bellum) and there must be right conduct within the war (jus in bello). Some Christian denominations, like the Mennonites, United Brethren, and Quakers have taken the position of pacifism, citing as their rationale that Jesus taught us how to die, not how to kill. This was, indeed, the position of the early Christian church for its first three hundred years.

The first believers would not fight for Caesar. After all, it was St. Paul who wrote,

> For we are not fighting against people…
>
> *Ephesians* 6:12 (LB)

But this is not what most Christian denominations have concluded over the past 1,700 years to be the biblical standard. The Bible says that life and justice are worth fighting for. The Scripture says:

> There is a time to kill, and a time to heal;
> A time for war, and a time for peace.
>
> *Ecclesiastes* 3:3, 8 (RSV)

> Remember the Lord, who is great and awesome, and fight for your brothers, your sons and your daughters, your wives and your homes.
>
> *Nehemiah* 4:14

Christianity and Judaism are not passive religions but aggressive. They maintain that there is such a thing as evil in the world that must be fought and defeated. God is not the least bit squeamish about death. To defeat evil He Himself was willing to pay the price of death upon a cross.

One Tiny Voice

No doubt you've been affected by one of these five issues: abortion, suicide, capital punishment, mercy killing, and war. Together they serve as the backdrop for what Pope John Paul II used to refer to as the "culture of death" that infects much of the modern world. Clearly God is prejudiced in favor of life. The followers of Jesus are to offer His life and light to a dark and dying world. But of course the question is "What can I do, I'm just one person?" To answer this question President Ronald

Reagan shared the following story at the 1984 National Prayer Breakfast. He said,

> An ancient monk living in a little remote village, spending most of his time in prayer or tending the garden from which he obtained his sustenance ...thought he heard the voice of God telling him to go to Rome. Believing that he had heard, he set out. Weeks and weeks later, he arrived there, having traveled most of the way on foot. It was at a time of a festival in Rome. They were celebrating over the Goths. He followed a crowd into the Coliseum, and then, there in the midst of this great crowd, he saw the gladiators come forth, stand before the Emperor, and say, "We who are about to die salute you."
>
> And he realized they were going to fight to the death for the entertainment of the crowds. He cried out, "In the name of Christ, stop!" And his voice was lost in the tumult there in the great Coliseum.
>
> And as the games began, he made his way down through the crowd and climbed over the wall and dropped to the floor of the arena. Suddenly the crowds saw this scrawny little figure making his way out to the gladiators and saying over and over again, "In the name of Christ, stop!"
>
> And they thought it was part of the entertainment, and at first they were amused. But then, when they realized it wasn't, they grew belligerent and angry. And as he was pleading with the gladiators, "In the name of Christ, stop!" one of them plunged his sword into his body. And as he fell to the sand of the area in death, his last words were, "In the name of Christ, stop!"
>
> And suddenly, a strange thing happened. The gladiators stood looking at this tiny form lying in the sand. A silence fell over the Coliseum. And then, someplace up in the upper tiers, an individual made his way to an exit and left, and the others began to follow. And in the dead silence, everyone left the Coliseum. That was the last battle to the death between gladiators in the Roman

Coliseum. Never again did anyone kill or did men kill each other for the entertainment of the crowd.

One tiny voice that could hardly be heard above the tumult, "In the name of Christ, stop!" It is something we could be saying to each other throughout the world today.

Jesus Intensifies Commandment Six

Shifting from the Old Testament to the New, you might assume that Jesus would relax the strident tone of the Sixth Commandment. After all, Jesus is presumed to be merciful. But rather than relax the command's requirement, Jesus escalates it. In His Sermon on the Mount Jesus says,

> Under the laws of Moses the rule was, "If you murder, you must die." But I have added to that rule, and tell you that if you are only angry, even in your own home, you are in danger of judgment!
>
> *Mathew* 5:21–22 (LB)

Jesus elevates the standard of the Sixth Commandment by connecting murder to anger. Murder is anger out of control. This was certainly true in John Brunner's case (the story at the beginning of this chapter). Evidently he got angry enough to kill his very own mother, which is not as uncommon as you might think. Every year thousands of family members murder each other in a fit of rage.

Anger is commonly expressed in four different ways. Some people *explode.* Others *go silent.* The exploder's anger is red hot, but the mute's anger is ice cold. Some people swallow all their anger and blame themselves for everything. These are the *depressed* angry. Their anger is turned in upon themselves, and they wind up chronically depressed. Finally, there is the *manipulating* angry. These are those who know just what buttons to push to get other people to explode for them. Each of these expressions are potential killers. They can kill both the one who is angry as well as the one who is the object of their anger. Jesus warns that such anger is just as damnable as murder itself. The Scripture counsels,

> It is better to have *self-control* than to control an army.
>
> *Proverbs* 16:32 (LB)

Keep in mind that God designed you to get angry from time to time. If you don't get angry over assaults upon women, the abuse of children, and the exploitation of the poor, then you are either insensitive or uncaring. The issue is not if you get angry, but how to express it appropriately. After all, anger can be deadly, as my friend John Brunner discovered.

Envy, the Root of Murder

Scripture does not stop with anger as a particular cause for murder. The Bible also cautions against envy. Here is how the apostle James expresses it:

> You want what you don't have, so you kill…
>
> *James* 4:2 (LB)

Cain murdered Abel, David had Uriah killed, and Jezebel arranged Naboth's death all out of envy! Over and over again the Bible cautions that envy is a principle cause of murder.

You may look enviously at those who appear to enjoy the perfect home, in the perfect neighborhood, with two perfect cars, and the two perfect children in the perfect schools. To secure such blessings you may over work and eventually kill the very family life you wanted to bless. The Scripture warns against envy—beware! The Bible testifies that the very first murder was a murder of envy!

Conclusion

As clear as the Sixth Commandment is, nonetheless the Bible does *not* declare murder to be an unpardonable sin. If you've killed your marriage with hated anger or cold silence, or if you've strangled your family life with overwork and striving, or if you've aborted your baby, or if you've murdered someone in a fit of passion like John Brunner, still there is *hope!*

Did you know that nearly half of the Bible was written by murderers? The first five books of the Bible are credited to Moses, who murdered an Egyptian guard in cold blood. (Exodus 2:12). Half the Psalms were written by King David, and he cunningly arranged the murder of Bathsheba's husband (2 Samuel 11). St. Paul was a killer. Before becoming a follower of Christ, he aggressively arrested believers for execution (Acts 8:1–3). So, if you've killed—whether directly or indirectly, take heart, because you share a lot in common with some of the Bible's greatest saints: Moses, King David, and St. Paul! God transformed them and gave them peace. God can do the very same for you!

The gospel of Jesus Christ provides power—enough spiritual power to unload the guilt of any sin. You may counter that sinful indiscretions are one thing, but a murder cannot be undone. Perhaps so, but remember, Jesus Himself was a murder victim. His execution was a cold-blooded decision on the part of the authorities in Jerusalem. He was murdered plain and simple. So Jesus knows all about murder, but His death wasn't final. It wasn't the last word. After He was crucified, dead, and buried, He returned to life for one express purpose! To forgive and bless. Murder is serious business to be sure, but so is grace. Death is not final. It is never the last word! Amen.

Study Guide: He Murdered His Mother!

90 minutes

Introduction (5 minutes)

Briefly

Have each participant vote with their feet …have them go to one end of the room if they believe they are capable of murder and to the other end of the room if they presume that they are not. Have each group explain their position.

*Opening Discussion/Warm Up(*10 *minutes)*

Have participants share stories of individuals they know personally who have been somehow connected to a murder (friend of a victim, police, insurance agent, newspaper reporter, neighbor …)

*Life Is Sacred!(*15 *minutes)*

According to Genesis 9, why is each individual's life sacred?

> Whoever sheds the blood of man, by man shall his blood be shed; *for God made man in his own image.*
>
> *Genesis* 9:6

According to Genesis 4:7 what was God's warning to Cain *before* he murdered his brother?

What does it mean to have sin "crouching at our door"?

According to Genesis 4:7 is sin aggressive or passive?

How do you "master" it?

*What The Law Does Not Say(*10 *minutes)*

Does God's law forbid all killing?

Specifically, what kind of killing is outlawed by God? Read Exodus 21:14.

> If a man willfully attacks another to kill him treacherously, you shall take him from my altar, that he may die.
>
> *Exodus* 21:14

Read Deuteronomy 21, which consists of biblical principles for making war.

Read Exodus 21:12–17, which consists of biblical principles for capital punishment.

Do the above verses suggest that God is squeamish about the killing of a human being? Is that still true today?

Five Modern Applications (25 minutes)

You probably don't fuss much about the Sixth Commandment. You may presume to have progressed beyond its concern. But there are five specific issues that confound everyone today involving the Sixth Commandment, and they are:

A. abortion,
B. suicide,
C. mercy killing,
D. capital punishment,
E. war.

Clearly the principle of the Sixth Commandment is simple, but its application isn't. Do you believe that God wants us to be "confident" when it comes to taking another person's life?

Jesus Escalates Commandment Six(10 minutes)

Typically, we assume that Jesus softens the strictness of the Old Testament law. Is this true when it comes to the Sixth Commandment?

> Under the laws of Moses the rule was, "If you murder, you must die." But I have added to that rule, and tell you that if you are only angry, even in your own home, you are in danger of judgment!
>
> *Matthew* 5:21–22 (LB)

Why does Jesus link anger with murder?

According to Jesus, are we never to get angry? Did He? See John 2:13–17.

Envy, the Root of Murder(20 minutes)

Read the passage from James:

> You want what you don't have, so you kill to get it.
>
> *James* 4:2 (LB)

According to James, what is the inevitable end of envy?

Conclusion(20 minutes)

Name some of the Bible's greatest saints who were also murderers?

- A. Exodus 2:11–12
- B. 2 Samuel 11:14–15
- C. Acts 9:1

If God can forgive, restore, and sanctify men like Moses, David, and St. Paul is there any reason why He could not do the same for someone who has killed today?

Application: According to Jennifer O'Neill in her book *You're Not Alone,* 43 percent of all U.S. women who have reached the age of forty-five years have had an abortion. Based on what we've studied are mercy, restoration, and peace available for those who have had an abortion?

Wrap Up (10 minutes)

Share your prayer requests with one another.

Confirm the date and location of the next meeting.

Close by reading out loud the following prayer.

Dear God,

Some of us have killed a marriage. Some of us have choked the life out of our family. Some murdered reputations and friendships. Some have ended the life of an unborn child, and others have killed in battle. Lord, forgive us. We cannot possibly make up for the loss, but in the fullness of time, You can raise new life out of death. May we trust You enough to take You at Your word when You say to each of us, "though your sins are like scarlet, they shall be as white as snow..." Amen.

Command Seven:
What Would Jesus Say to the Adulterer?

Bud and Martha's fiftieth wedding anniversary packed their church's fellowship hall. From all over the country, family and friends flew in to celebrate. The ring of laughter resounded as fifty years of stories were shared. Amid the celebration, however, one story cast a shadow. It was the affair. Twenty-two years earlier, Bud had left home for another woman. Everyone knew all about it. Indeed, most of the guests had been actors in that painful drama; they had listened to Martha's fury and tears. They had helped with the kids as needed. They had visited with Bud to listen to him and better understand his perspective. Family and friends did what they could to be supportive during the eighteen-month ordeal. It was an anxious and tormented time, all of which made the celebration of their fiftieth that much more remarkable. You see, those present for the anniversary celebration knew they had witnessed one of God's quiet miracles twenty two years ago; the resurrection of Bud and Martha's marriage from the dead. For this reason their fiftieth wedding anniversary had a kind of reverence to it—an acknowledgment that their marriage somehow had God's fingerprints upon it. No one felt the need to talk about Bud's affair that day because quite simply there was something more profound over which to rejoice—a marriage with God's fingerprints all over it.

We come to what many consider the least popular of the Ten Commandments.

> You shall not commit adultery.
>
> *Exodus* 20:12

The Seventh Commandment is the juiciest—the one that inspires the most titillation. We are both appalled and fascinated by those who break it: Prince Charles and Lady Di, A-Rod and Madonna, presidents Clinton and Kennedy, and of course the cast of thousands in Hollywood. For all the attention this command gets one would think that we would have overcome its temptation by now, but the statistics reveal just the opposite. Adultery is an open wound in our culture.

But first, let's set the record straight—breaking the Seventh Commandment is not the most damnable offense. The reason the Seventh Commandment is violated is because the First Commandment is already broken—the command that says, "Thou shalt have no other gods before Me!" In a typical affair, personal pleasure eclipses God. Feelings overshadow faith. Make no mistake, you break the Seventh Commandment because you have already done something more serious—you've broken the First Commandment. You've allowed something (or someone) to come between you and God.

But as in Bud's case there is hope for the adulterer. God has a way of taking turning our worst mistakes, and redeeming them into a surprise of joy. Nothing is more heartbreaking than the revelation of unfaithfulness within a marriage, and yet nothing is more wondrous than the restoration of marital trust. God can do this. Remember, God Himself is victim to countless spiritual adulteries as men and women chase after other gods. Nonetheless, God redeems broken trust, just as He did with Bud and Mary Martha. He can do it for you too!

Christ and Culture

According to Peggy Vaughan, author of *The Monogamy Myth,* 60 percent of men and 40 percent of women will have an affair at some point in their marriage! This statistic doesn't mean that husbands and wives are secretly enjoying a good time. What it means is that millions of individuals are suffering serious emotional and psychological pain—enough pain to risk their marriages, their families, their reputations, and their personal integrity. Adultery is often a desperate attempt to cope with pain.

Adultery is also an indication that American culture is undisciplined and self-centered. More and more people are now convinced that sex is not only natural but necessary. They're convinced that to confine sex to marriage is needlessly repressive, and that to restrain your natural sex drive is to do yourself harm. This point of view is of course popular. But it implies that passion is more important than principle for mental and emotional health. The facts, however, don't confirm it. A study done at the University of Tennessee found a "direct correlation between illicit sexual behavior and serious emotional problems." The folly of unrestrained passions is also confirmed by the steady disintegration of American marriages and the rise of all manner of neuroses and psychoses. Simply put, many today are *lost* when it comes to love—they don't have the faintest idea of what love is, and how it functions martially, emotionally, and sexually.

Today's culture tends to define love as a feeling, but the Bible does not. Indeed, the Bible defines love quite unemotionally. It says:

> Love is patient and kind; love is not jealous and boastful; it is not arrogant or rude. Love does not insist on its own way; it is not irritable or resentful; it does not rejoice

> at wrong, but rejoices in the right. Love bears all things, believes all things, hopes all things, endures all things.
>
> 1 *Corinthians* 13:4–7 *(*RSV*)*

Notice, there is no mention of feelings here whatsoever. That's because the Bible is less than impressed when it comes to feelings. It knows that your feelings are dependent upon circumstances. How you feel about somebody is influenced by how much they weigh, what they wear, how much money they have, and how much you've had to drink. But love as the Bible defines it is unconditional—it is above and beyond your feelings!

Genesis tells the story of Joseph, who served as the chief household slave in the home of Potiphar, a rich and powerful Egyptian general. Potiphar trusted Joseph. Indeed, he entrusted his entire household into Joseph's care whenever he was away. Now Joseph was young and very handsome, and Potiphar's wife wanted him in her bed. Time and again she enticed him to sleep with her, but Joseph refused. By our standards today Joseph was a fool. After all, an affair with Potifar's wife could be easily justified. Joseph was a slave, confined against his will. What better way to express all his pent-up frustration than to enjoy his master's wife. What's more, didn't he have needs? Didn't he too have feelings? Didn't he have a right to be a man even if he was a slave!? But Joseph didn't give in to his feelings. Instead, he said to Potiphar's wife,

> How could I …sin against God?
>
> *Genesis* 39:9

Notice how Joseph made his decision. He based it upon what he believed instead of how he felt! Beware any time when your feelings begin to overshadow your faith …when your personal needs threaten to eclipse your creeds. That's when big compromises are made and when personal integrity is sold to satisfy a fleeting impulse.

How often we hear from men and women in the middle of an affair, "But it feels so right." I remember when Bud used to say this to me in the middle of his affair. He would say it with a passionate conviction, " …it feels so right." But just because he felt good didn't mean everyone else did. His wife, children, and family were positively sick.

Popular culture may wrap both arms around the notion that feelings are what are most important, but God remains unmoved. His word on adultery remains firm and clear.

> …Let the marriage bed be undefiled; for God will judge the immoral and adulterous.
>
> *Hebrews* 13:4 (RSV)

Today you can get a sympathetic hearing for why an affair is legitimate. You're lonely and tired. Your marriage bed is cold. Your stress is unbearable. As I said, you can come up with countless reasons for why your affair is justified. But remember, when you do you're betting the farm that you are right and that God is wrong. Essentially, what you are saying is that you know better what is right, true, and healthy than God does, which is exactly what the Bible defines to be sin. Sin is when we declare ourselves right and God either outdated, out of touch, or out of your life. Again, to rationalize an affair is to bet the farm that God is wrong when He says:

> Adultery will cost a man all he has.
>
> *Proverbs* 6:26 (GN)

When Bud woke up to the fact that he was about to lose everything that meant anything to him—his family, home, respect, and personally integrity, not to mention a good chunk of his savings and personal retirement account, he quickly put an end to his affair and returned home. Fortunately, his wife Martha had invested countless prayers to keep her heart open. Most wayward husbands are not so blessed.

Our culture is currently up for sale, and evidently advertisers know that the best way to sell it is through sex. But God's position on adultery is resolute: "Thou shalt not commit adultery!"

A friend of mine who is a musician in Miami learned this lesson the hard way. His wife wasn't so forgiving when he wanted to return home after his affair. He now lives hand to mouth after forking over the house and a large portion of his personal and retirement savings. Every month he must transfer thousands of dollars into his ex-wife's account in alimony and childcare payments! He works twice as hard and enjoys half as much money ! The bill collectors call him constantly, keeping him company at night. *Remember!* When you break God's laws, they break you!

The Wedding Vow

Here it's instructive to review the wedding vow in order to remind you that feelings had nothing to do with the promise you make on your wedding day. This is what the classic Christian wedding vow says.

> I, _____, take you, _____
> To be my wedded wife/husband
> To have and to hold,
> From this day forward,
> For better, for worse,
> For richer, for poorer,
> In sickness and in health,
> To love and to cherish
> Till death do us part.

Notice that the vow says absolutely nothing about feelings. It doesn't promise you will love your husband or wife as long as they look good, or as long as you still have romantic feelings toward them, or as long as the marriage is financially viable. people say to pastors all the time, "But I've fallen out of love with him or her." So what! That wasn't the promise you made when you exchanged vows on your wedding day. The vow was that you would do loving things for them; that you would work for what was best for them, in good times and in bad; for better or worse; for richer or poorer; in sickness or health. The wedding vow is not an expression of how you feel; it is a promise to commit yourself to the other person no matter what happens—regardless of the circumstances. She may gain fifty pounds. He may become a drunk. Nonetheless, the wedding vow promises your commitment to them regardless. This is what makes the Christian wedding vow so terrifyingly awesome. In it you do not pledge your feelings but your faithfulness. As a Christian you choose to be led by principles not by passions, by commitments not by compulsions, by beliefs not by feelings. Adultery is all about satisfying your own needs regardless of who is impacted: children, colleagues, friends, and family members. Marriage, however, is to consciously choose to honor all those commitments.

This, by the way, is a reason why the Bible counsels so strongly to choose your marriage partner wisely. "Do not be unequally yoked," the Bible prescribes. In other words, be smart in how you choose, because adultery is just too costly.

Christ and Cause

The book of Proverbs cautions,

> Adultery is a trap…
>
> *Proverbs* 22:14 (GN)

I doubt you've met anyone who told you, "Yea, I got involved in an affair, and now my life is so much better!" In twenty-six years as a pastor, I've seen individuals lose their families, homes, friends, reputations, and big chunks of their paychecks all because of an affair. So the obvious question is: "If it is so disastrous, how does it start?" After all, no one wakes up in the morning and says to themselves, "I think I'll start that affair today." Like the Bible says, an affair is a trap that we fall into. We don't choose it. We fall into it.

Keep in mind this simple principle. "*It starts in the head, not in bed.*" Adultery always starts inside the running conversation of our own private thoughts. As the Scripture says:

> Evil thoughts lead to evil actions.
>
> *James* 1:15 (LB)

Jesus Himself knew it started in the head. After all, it was He who said,

> You have heard that it was said, "You shall not commit adultery." But I say to you that everyone who looks at a woman lustfully has already committed adultery with her in his heart.
>
> *Matthew* 5:27–28 (RSV)

God's commandment against adultery involves more than a physical prohibition against sex with someone who is married because adultery occurs first in the mind, and then in the body. It does us no good to rationalize, "Well, I looked, but I didn't touch." Jesus cautions that what goes on in your mind is just as damning as what you do with your body. The Lord calls you to a higher standard. You are not to merely avoid fornicating with another married person. You are to honor your marriage mind, heart, soul, and body!

Christ and Compassion

But what about those who have already fallen, who have already allowed a third person to interrupt their marriage? Make no mistake, God is not mocked. Judgment is swift and sure. The Scripture is clear:

> God will judge the adulterer.
>
> *Hebrews* 13:4

But this need not be the final word. When reading the New Testament Jesus is especially sympathetic with those who fall into sexual sin. In the eighth chapter of the Gospel of John an adulterous women was brought before Jesus. She had been caught in bed with a man who was not her husband and thrown naked in the dust before the Lord. Her accusers reminded Him that the law of Moses declared adultery to be punishable with death by stoning. Leviticus 20:10 says,

> If a man commits adultery with the wife of his neighbor, both the adulterer and the adulteress shall be put to death.
>
> *Leviticus* 20:10 (NRSV)

But Jesus responded by saying, "Let he who is without sin cast the first stone." One by one, beginning with the oldest, they dropped their stones, and left, until Jesus was left alone with the terrified woman. He said to her, "Woman, is there no one left to accuse you?"

And she said, "No one, Lord."

"Then neither do I accuse you." He said, "But go, and do not sin again!"

Jesus is sympathetic toward those who fall into sexual sin. But His forgiveness comes with the caution, "Go, and do not sin again!" The reason He is so adamant about not falling into the same sin is found in Proverbs 6:32:

> A man who commits adultery doesn't have any sense.
> He is just destroying himself.
>
> *Proverbs* 6:32 (GN)

Jesus is stern, not for His sake but for your own. He knows that adultery is self-destructive. It not only destroys families and friendships, it destroys the two individuals involved from the inside out. Self-respect is lost along with personal integrity. And more importantly, it disconnects you from God, for as was mentioned at the start, to break the Seventh Commandment is to first break the First Commandment—it is to allow someone to get between you and God.

Application

If you are currently involved in an affair, the first thing that you need to do is to stop and ask God for help. This may seem counter-intuitive—asking God for help with an affair. But if God helped only those who deserved it, He wouldn't help anyone.

Next, end the affair immediately. Don't do it gradually … savoring just one more time together. You need to end it, politely if possible or impolitely if necessary.

Finally, you must do whatever it takes to stay away from the partner of your affair. If this requires you to quit your job, sell your house and move to another country, do it. Your marriage and your family are more important than a house, a job, and even your bank balance. You can get another career, you can buy another house, and you can replenish your bank account, but you cannot enjoy your family as God intended while living in two different houses. Your marriage is worth protecting, and it is worth making sacrifices for.

Conclusion

When Bud finally returned home to Martha, it wasn't easy. The issues that led to the affair were still there, and in addition there was a mountain of hurt feelings to overcome. But if Bud and Martha had learned anything through the ordeal, it was that love is more profound than any particular feeling—good or bad. Love steers you clear of foolish impulses, and helps you scale mountains of bitterness, resentment, and even hatred. Love, the Bible tells us, is the only thing that truly lasts. Resentments will fade, bitterness wears out, and even our hatreds are eventually forgotten, but love—true love—will endure. It is just as the Bible promises:

> Love bears all things, believes all things, hopes all things, endures all things. Love never ends.
>
> 1 Corinthians 13:7 (RSV)

Most guests at Bud's and Martha's fiftieth wedding anniversary hadn't given their marriage much hope when Bud returned home after his eighteen-month affair. At the time we all said things like "It will never survive," "She'll throw the bum out," and "He doesn't deserve her." But then we all witnessed one of God's quiet miracles unfold—the resurrection of a dead marriage. This is why we flew in from all over the country to celebrate. To honor God's death defying power. To marvel again at a marriage with God's fingerprints all over it. Amen.

Study Guide: What Would Jesus Say to the Adulterer?

90 minutes

Introduction (10 minutes)

Briefly

Cut out pictures from magazines of Hollywood couples whose marriage is in the news and share them with the group. What is the overarching message Hollywood communicates about marriage and adultery? How much does this message influence our culture?

Opening Discussion/Warm Up(5 minutes)

Have participants share their experiences of attending a fiftieth wedding anniversary. What was the overarching message communicated at such celebrations?

Christ and Culture (15 minutes)

According to Peggy Vaughan, author of *The Monogamy Myth,* 60 percent of men and 40 percent of woman will have an affair at some point in their marriage! Does this statistic mean that husbands and wives are secretly enjoying a good time or does it mean that they are in pain?

More and more people are now convinced that sex is not only natural but necessary, that to restrain your natural sex drive is to do yourself harm. Is this true, or is it true that illicit sexual behavior breeds emotional trouble?

Have the group read aloud together 1 Corinthians 13. Does this chapter define love as a feeling? How does 1 Corinthians 13 define love? What implication does this have for marital sex?

What is God's basic sexual standard within marriage?

> Let the marriage bed be undefiled; for God will judge the immoral and adulterous.
>
> *Hebrews* 13:4

According to Scripture, how expensive is adultery?

> Adultery will cost a man all he has.
>
> *Proverbs* 6:26

The Wedding Vow (10 minutes)

Ask if anyone in the group can recite their wedding vow by heart. If not, have the group read together the traditional wedding vow

> I, _____, take you, _____
> To be my wedded wife/husband
> To have and to hold,
> From this day forward,
> For better, for worse,
> For richer, for poorer,
> In sickness and in health,
> To love and to cherish
> Till death do us part.

Does the wedding vow make any promises involving your feelings?

What exactly is the traditional wedding vow promising?

The Bible counsels, "Do not be unequally yoked with an unbeliever." In other words, don't get married or mixed up with someone who does not follow Christ! What about this counsel is wise?

Christ and Cause(20 *minutes*)

What is meant when the Bible says,

> Adultery is a trap...
>
> *Proverbs* 22:14 (GN)

According to Hebrews 13:4, is God easy going when it comes to adultery?

Break up into same-sex teams and come up with slogans that communicate the principle: "It starts in head, not in bed."

Did Jesus soften God's standard on sex?

> You have heard that it was said, "You shall not commit adultery." But I say to you that everyone who looks at a woman lustfully has already committed adultery with her in his heart.
>
> *Matthew* 5:27–28

Christ and Compassion (20 *minutes*)

Review the Old Testament standard on punishing adultery.

> If a man commits adultery with the wife of his neighbor, both the adulterer and the adulteress shall be put to death.
>
> *Leviticus* 20:10

Read out loud the story of Jesus and the adulterous woman—John 8:2–11.

Why did the woman's accusers drop their stones and walk away?

What were Jesus's last words to the woman? Why?

> He who commits adultery has no sense;
> He who does it destroys himself.
>
> *Proverbs* 6:23

Wrap Up (10 minutes)

Share your prayer requests with one another.

Confirm the date and location of the next meeting.

Close by reading out loud the following prayer.

Dear God,

You've created us for marriage, but marriage is much more demanding and difficult than we ever imagined. Sometimes it can be painful, and we look for comfort. Sometimes it can be frustrating, and we look for consolation. Sometimes it can feel dead, and we look for life. Lord, save us from any temptation that would take us away from our marriage. Give us the love we require to endure the hard times. And supply us with the hope that will reassure us that the good times with our spouse are not lost forever, but will return better than ever. Lord, give us the desire to make any and all changes we must make in ourselves for the sake of our spouse. As husbands, help us to love our wives. As wives, help us to respect our husbands. And Lord, when we are tempted to give up, remind us that You never give up on us.

Into Your hands, Lord, I commit my marriage! Amen.

Command Eight:
Integrity Is Worth More

Jan Baker saw herself as an honest woman. She believed in telling the truth, paying her bills, and doing the right thing. She thought everyone else should do the same. But then she and her husband fell behind on their credit card payments. *No big deal,* she thought to herself. She would tame the family finances with more disciplined spending and conscientious bill paying. But then her family got hit with some emergency medical expenses. Creditors soon began calling, which was humiliating, but Jan soldiered on and did the best she could. She and her husband worked all the overtime possible and cut all nonessential expenses. Still, with each passing month, the family got further behind, and she could feel the approach of a financial meltdown. There wasn't any obvious solution, but there was a handy one which Jan did her best never to consider. You see, Jan worked for a building materials company as an account clerk. Part of her responsibility was to oversee the company's petty cash account—money given to company truckers to pay for highway tolls, diesel fuel, and other incidental expenses. There was always at least $1,000 in small bills in the account box, and Jan was in charge of it. She could easily borrow some of the cash, cover her tracks by writing fake receipts, and then pay it all back the following month. Jan never gave the money a second thought, but then the bank threatened to repossess her car. The next day she took $234 from the petty cash box and wrote a fake receipt for diesel fuel. She pledged in her heart that she would pay it back, and indeed she maintained a careful record of what she took. But instead of paying the company back the following month, Jan took another $173. She felt ashamed, but she also felt as if she was at the end of her rope. She wasn't abusive with the liberty she took. Only in desperation did she take anything, and always, always she promised herself to pay it back with interest. But she wasn't able. Mercifully, no one at work ever discovered her theft.

We come now to the Eighth Commandment.

> You shall not steal.
>
> *Exodus* 20:15

It is amazing how consistently this precept is proclaimed throughout the world. For example, a proverb from a traditional African religion says,

> Where you did not sow, do not reap.

China's Tao says,

> To take …unrighteous wealth is like satisfying one's hunger with putrid food …It gives …temporary relief, but death also follows …Taoism.
>
> *Treatise on Response and Retribution,* 5

The Qur'an of Islam states ominously,

> As for the thief, both male and female, cut off their hands.
>
> *Qur'an* 5:38

There are, of course, different kinds of stealing. Synonyms for stealing are to swindle, shoplift, hustle, rip off, forge, smuggle, mooch, sneak, plagiarize, and poach. There is blue-collar stealing such as pick-pocketing and armed robbery, and there is white-collar stealing such as money laundering and insider trading. There is the stealing of money, possessions, and ideas. There is the theft of one's reputation. Finally, there is the theft of time—when we are robbed of precious moments by the inconsiderate who make us wait.

The difference between the thief and the honest dealer is actually quite small, for both want the same thing—both want what is good, beautiful, and valuable. The difference is only in approach. The honest individual will work and wait for what they want, but the thief wants immediate gratification. Again, the difference between the honest individual and the thief is not in what they want, but how they go about getting it.

The Miami Herald published a story about the wife of a St. Paul, Minnesota, dentist who was sentenced to jail in a "shoplifting for hire" case. The story goes that Judy Dick hired a personal shoplifter to steal $7,000 worth of department store items. Apparently, she wrote out a detailed list of the things that she wanted to "order" from her shoplifter, and he went to the store "to pick them up." Now here's the principle—Judy Dick wasn't wrong to want beautiful and expensive things. What was wrong was her approach—she was not willing to work and wait so that she could pay for them.

I like what David Seamands wrote many years ago about stealing and its relationship to working and waiting.

> Stealing is getting the reward without paying the price, collecting the dividend without making the investment. It's receiving money without working, it making good grades without studying; it's trying for the top of the ladder without climbing the rungs. Life involves putting something

> into it and receiving something in return. Stealing, however, is the shortcut philosophy of life that contradicts this basic principle of the universe.[4]

Ethical shortcuts may yield short-term gains, but it is integrity that pays off in the end. As the Scriptures says,

> Ill-gotten gain brings no lasting happiness;
> right living does.
>
> *Proverbs* 10:2 (LB)

In this chapter I'll examine some of the Eighth Commandment's most practical applications. Let me start with the most basic application of all—we are not to steal from God!

Don't Steal from God!

There were three prevailing economic philosophies that guided the 20th century: capitalism, communism, and Christianity. Capitalism maintained that all money and possessions were personal—owned by the individual. Communism said that all money and possessions were public—owned by the state. Christianity, however, claimed that all money and possessions were God's. After all, the Bible says:

> The Earth is the Lord's and everything in it.
>
> *Psalm* 24:1

> The silver is mine, and the gold is mine, declares the Lord Almighty.
>
> *Haggai* 2:8

According to the Bible, personal and/or public ownership is an illusion. Again the Scripture says,

> For we brought nothing into this world, and it is certain that we can carry nothing out.
>
> 1 *Timothy* 6:7 (KJV)

You may resist this idea, reasoning you've worked hard for what you have, but the deeper reality is that it all comes from God. Your life, health, energy, and ability—all the human capacities that make it possible for you to acquire what you have—they all come from God. The Lord is the source of all things.

Please follow my reasoning closely here. If it all comes from God then you are a caretaker for what you have and God is the real owner. You are a trustee. Therefore, you are to use the things that God entrusts to you according to His purposes and priorities.

Allow me a fanciful illustration. If Microsoft's Bill Gates were to entrust a portion of his personal wealth and estate to your care, I'm confident Mr. Gates would give specific instructions for how to manage it all. If you ignored his instructions and used his wealth for your own purposes, he would be right to arrest you for stealing.

Let's change this illustration just a bit by changing the name of the estate owner from Bill Gates to God. God entrusts a portion of His estate to you with specific instructions for how to manage it. If you ignore His instructions and instead manage His property your way for your own purposes, once again, you would be guilty of stealing.

The last book of the Old Testament speaks to this very circumstance. The prophet Malachi accuses the people of Israel of stealing from God because they did not handle God's possessions according to His explicit instructions. For example, followers of God are instructed to give generously to three specific causes:

1. God's ministry
2. the poor
3. God's people who are in need.

How much is to be given? God's minimum standard is 10 percent—the tithe. God's followers are to give at least ten percent of everything they earn. If you don't tithe then God charges you with stealing. God knows Himself to be the rightful owner of everything, and when you don't manage God's things His way then as far as God is concerned you are stealing. The prophet Malachi says,

> Will anyone rob God? Yet you are robbing (Him)! But you say, "How are we robbing (Him)?" In your tithes and offerings.
>
> *Malachi* 3:8 *(*NRSV*)*

God gives specific instructions for how to manage His creation. Among these instructions is the principle that people are to give generously. Indeed, God is so fanatical about this principle that He invites you to put Him to the test. He says,

> Bring the full amount of your tithes ...Put me to the test and you will see that I will open the windows of heaven and pour out on you an abundance of all kinds of good things.
>
> *Malachi* 3:10 *(*GN*)*

This is the only place in all of scripture where God specifically invites you to put Him to the test—in your generosity. Naturally, people find this principle difficult. They fear that if they give away 10 percent that they will not have enough for themselves. But God promises just the opposite. To those who give, God promises an abundant blessing—"I will open the windows of heaven and pour out on you an abundance of all kinds of good things."

Again, the twentieth century was influenced by three major economic philosophies: capitalism, communism, and Christianity. Capitalism directed its followers to make as much money as possible, and to give away the leftovers. Communism directed it followers to give everything to the state, so that the state could be charitable. Christianity directed its followers differently. John Welsey in his sermon "The Use of Money" wrote, "Make all you can. Save all you can. Give all you can." Those who followed this principle always had more than enough. Indeed, they had enough to share.

The Eighth Commandment directs believers not to steal, and the first person they are not to steal from is God.

Don't Steal from Your Neighbor

We are also not to steal from others!

Mark Twain once wrote,

> When I was a boy I was walking along the street when I happened to spy a cart full of watermelons. I was fond of watermelon, so I sneaked up quietly and snitched one. I ran to a nearby alley and sank my teeth into it, but no sooner had I done so, however, when a strange feeling came over me, and without a moment's hesitation I walked back to the cart, replaced the melon, and stole a ripe one.

Yes, there is something perverse in us that enjoys taking what is not ours. As the Scripture says,

> Stolen water is sweet.
>
> *Proverbs* 9:17 (NRSV)

Children aren't taught to steal; they don't have to be. They do it quite instinctively. Parents know the shock of discovering the theft of their young child—the candy taken from the store, the toy snitched from a neighbor's house, the money pilfered from the parent's wallet. They can barely talk, yet they know how to steal! There is something about what is stolen that is "sweet."

Those we steal from most are our employers. Employee theft costs our economy billions and billions of dollars every year, and of course this mountain of theft must be compensated for with higher prices. This theft is justified with the rationale that the stock room is so full that one missing item will mean nothing. But to this the Scripture says,

> Whatever you do, work at it with all your heart, as working for the Lord.
>
> *Colossians* 3:23 (GN)

You are to work for your employer as if working for the Lord Himself. And you are not to rationalize stealing as Jan did when she promised herself that she would pay back the money she "borrowed."

The government is another major victim of stealing. The IRS estimates that unpaid taxes costs our country over 200 billion dollars a year. The Scripture says,

> The authorities are working for God …Pay what you owe them; pay your personal and property taxes…
>
> *Romans* 13:6–7 (GN)

Another kind of stealing is unpaid loans. Sadly, the number one kind of unpaid loan is to a family member or friend. This includes everything from tapes and tools, to cash and cars. Long-term borrowing when not repaid is the same as stealing, and the Scripture cautions,

> The wicked borrow and never pay back…
>
> *Psalm* 37:21 (GN)

We are all born with an instinct to take what is not ours. Some do it maliciously as premeditated theft. Others do it thoughtlessly by simply not returning what was borrowed. Obviously motives are important, but in the end whether we rob a neighbor of his tools or simply neglect to return them, the effect is the same—the neighbor loses. God's standard is clear—we are not to take what is not ours.

The Rich Stealing from the Poor

Let's keep in mind that the Scripture has much harsher words for the "haves" who take from the "have nots." It's easy to beat up on the little guy for petty theft. But infinitely more damage is done to the social fabric by the privileged who take advantage of the less fortunate.

On April 16, 2009, the new Yankee Stadium was unveiled. Tickets were as high as $2,625 a seat. That kind of money is of course needed to support a team whose payroll is over 200 million dollars. And of course the new stadium itself cost over 1.5 billion dollars. As one commentator said, the stadium itself is a monument to excess. Jeff Passan of Yahoo! Sports openly asked in his column if "deep down, beneath the Yankee moneymaking behemoth, could there exist the slightest sense of guilt?" Every minute a child dies somewhere in the world of starvation, but Yankee Stadium is plush. Here is my point. In the coming years families will be enticed by savvy Yankees marketing to visit the new Yankee Stadium and *charge onto their credit cards an evening of baseball that they cannot afford.* As one fan said who attended the stadium's opening day commented, "I knew when I came here I was going to spend a bunch of money I didn't have." The dictionary has a word for this—exploitation.

The Bible reserves stern words for those who exploit the less fortunate, especially the poor.

> Do not exploit the poor …for the Lord will take up their case and will plunder those who plunder them.
>
> *Proverbs* 22:22–23

The economic reality of our world today is this: the top 1 percent of the world's wealthy control more resources than the bottom 90 percent. The global economy is heavily influenced by a small oligarchy of ownership who mixes their money with politics to control much of the global agenda. The Bible has a simple word for this—injustice. Sharing is a biblical imperative, and in a world where three billion people live on less than two dollars a day it is biblically immoral to have Fortune 500 officers earning eight million dollars annually. Of course, much of the stealing that the rich do occurs openly in the marketplace via insider trading, sweetheart deals, stock options, and golden parachutes. What's more, corporations are masters at stealing from "Joe Six Pack." These businesses employ the brightest marketing minds money can buy to dream up ways to entice Joe Six Pack to…

> Buy things he doesn't need
> with money he doesn't have
> to impress people he doesn't know.

The modern marketplace has run amuck with the strong cashing in on the weak. The poor are not held up at gunpoint, but their money winds up in the pockets of the rich just the same. The Eighth Commandment is more than just a protection of property. When it commands, "Thou shalt not steal," it warns against leveraging those who are easily exploited. We are all accountable to God, rich and poor alike. But even a casual read through Scripture is enough to convince any reasonable soul that God has a bias for the poor. What's more, God scrutinizes the rich. Indeed, He goes so far as to say,

> It is easier for a camel to go through the eye of a needle than for the rich man to enter the kingdom of God.
>
> *Matthew* 19:24

Simply put, the rich are not to take advantage of the poor. The Bible considers it the same as stealing. It offers a curse to the dishonest and a promise to those who remain upright.

> Wealth you get by dishonesty will do you no good, but honesty can save your life.
>
> *Proverbs* 10:2 (GN)

The Bible is clear that we are not to steal from God or from others. Finally, we are not to steal from ourselves!

Don't Steal from Yourself

Jan Baker's theft may never have been discovered, but still she had to live with herself, for as the Scripture cautions,

> You reap whatever you sow.
>
> *Galatians* 6:7 (NRSV)

People aren't born bad, nor do they go bad over night. Instead a slow erosion of personal integrity occurs each and every time they reach for what is not theirs. To steal is to rob from one's own integrity. The small transgressions we permit ourselves are what drive real character away.

This is what happened with Zacchaeus. The Gospel of Luke tells the story of Zacchaeus, who was the chief tax collector of Jericho. He was rich and hated. As chief tax collector he squeezed people for their money. Indeed, the Roman governor gave him the authority skim off the top whatever he raised over and above what the Romans demanded. He didn't consider it stealing, but the people of Jericho certainly did! One day Jesus came to town and drew a big crowd. Zacchaeus was curious to see Him, but he was too short to peer over the assembled crowd, so he climbed a sycamore tree to get a better view. When Jesus passed by He looked up and said, "Zacchaeus, hurry down, because I must stay in your house today." There is no record of what occurred next. What we do know is that their time together changed Zacchaeus. He changed from a powerful man who stole from the poor to a generous man who shared what he had with those in need. And this is what Zacchaeus promised to Jesus after their encounter.

> Look Sir, I will give half my property to the poor. And if I have swindled anybody out of anything I will pay him back four times as much.
>
> *Luke* 19:8 *(Phillips)*

The principle here is simple: spend any time with the Lord and you will be changed from a small-minded thief into a big-hearted benefactor. Indeed, this is just what happened to Jan Baker.

Redemption

Jan's theft never sat well in her soul. Years passed, and even though no one ever found out, still in her heart there wasn't any peace. Her family finances eventually straightened out, but she wasn't able to rest. So after years of gnawing guilt Jan decided to start saving. A little at first, but then more aggressively. Eventually, Jan saved and saved until she had enough to cover the money she had stolen plus interest. She then called her former employer and asked if she could pay him a visit. When she arrived at his home, she was nervous. She wasn't sure what to say or what to expect. There was the faint possibility that she could be arrested. Still she pressed forward because she wanted peace. Sitting in her former employer's library, she disclosed all that she had taken, handing him the detailed record she had kept. She then handed him in cash enough money to cover everything. Her former employer sat dumbfounded. It never occurred to him to have Jan arrested. Quite the opposite. He was deeply moved, and without hesitation he handed the money back. It was the freest moment of Jan's life.

Study Guide: Integrity Is Worth More

90 minutes

Introduction (10 minutes)

Briefly

Have each participant share their memory of their very first childhood theft.

Opening Discussion/Warm Up(5 minutes)

Break up into two groups: one group for those who were taught to steal by their parents, and a second group for those who were taught not to steal by their parents. Assuming everyone will gather in the second group, discuss from where the capacity to steal comes.

Define Stealing(5 minutes)

Read the following quote out loud together:

> Stealing is getting the reward without paying the price, collecting the dividend without making the investment. It's receiving money without working, it making good grades without studying; it's trying for the top of the ladder without climbing the rungs. Life involves putting something into it and receiving something in return. Stealing, however, is the shortcut philosophy of life that contradicts this basic principle of the universe.[5]
>
> David Seamends

Do those who steal and those who are honest want different things, or do they simply take a different approach to getting what they want? Why?

Stealing and Happiness(5 minutes)

The Scripture says:

> Ill-gotten gain brings no lasting happiness;
> right living does.
>
> *Proverbs* 10:2 (LB)

Have participants share personal examples or people they've witnessed that confirm the truth of this proverb.

Don't Steal from God(15 minutes)

The Bible claims that if you don't give 10 percent of your income to God's work in the world that you are stealing from Him! Read the following scripture out loud together:

> Will anyone rob God? Yet you are robbing me (says God)! But you say, "How are we robbing you?" In your tithes and offerings! You are cursed with a curse, for you are robbing me …Bring the full tithe (10 percent) into the storehouse…
>
> *Malachi* 3:8–10 (NRSV)

How fearful are you of tithing …giving 10 percent of your income to God's work for others? Are you afraid that if you give, you won't have enough for yourself?

Read out loud together God's promise to those who tithe:

> See if I will not open the windows of heaven for you and pour down for you an overflowing blessing.
>
> *Malachi* 3:10 (NRSV)

For those who are not tithing, do you think you could get started this year by giving 2 percent of your income to God's work in the world and then increasing your giving by 1 percent each year until you reach 10 percent? Will you commit to doing it?

Don't Steal from Others(15 minutes)

Mark Twain once wrote,

> When I was a boy I was walking along the street when I happened to spy a cart full of watermelons. I was fond of watermelon, so I sneaked up quietly and snitched one. I ran to a nearby alley and sank my teeth into it, but no sooner had I done so, however, when a strange feeling came over me, and without a moment's hesitation I walked back to the cart, replaced the melon, and stole a ripe one.

Have someone read the following verse:

> Stolen water is sweet.
>
> *Proverbs* 9:17 (NRSV)

Is there something perverse in us that enjoys taking what is not ours?

If we borrow something and never return it, are we stealing?

> The wicked borrow and never pay back…
>
> *Psalm* 37:21 (GN)

The Rich Stealing from the Poor(5 minutes)

Have someone read the following statement for the group:

> The modern marketplace has run amuck with the strong cashing in on the weak. The poor might not be held up at gunpoint, but their money winds up in the pockets of the rich just the same. The Eighth Commandment is more than just a protection of property. When it commands, "Thou shalt not steal," it warns against taking advantage of those who are easily exploited. We are all accountable to God, rich and poor alike. But even a casual read through Scripture is enough to convince any reasonable person that God has a bias for the poor.

Discuss amongst yourselves what is right and wrong about the above statement. Provide illustrations from the Bible where possible.

What do you think God means when He says:

> It is easier for a camel to go through the eye of a needle than for the rich man to enter the kingdom of God.
>
> *Matthew* 19:24

*Do Not Steal from Yourself(*15 *Minutes)*

Have someone read the following statement for the group:

> People aren't born bad, nor do they go bad over night. Instead a slow erosion of integrity occurs each and every time they reach for what is not theirs. To steal is to rob from one's own integrity. The large and small transgressions permitted are what drive real character away.

Discuss amongst yourselves what is right and wrong about the above statement.

Zacchaeus was the chief tax collector of Jericho (Luke 19:2). He was rich and hated. As chief tax collector he squeezed people for their money. Indeed, the Roman governor gave him the authority to raise as much in taxes as he could extort. He didn't consider it stealing, but the people of Jericho certainly did!

Read together the story of Zacchaeus (Luke 19:1–10). Discuss the state of Zacchaeus's integrity before and after he met with Jesus. What specifically did Zacchaeus do in response to spending time with the Lord?

*Redemption(*10 *minutes)*

Is it possible for God, not only to forgive our thefts, but to somehow use them for good? Was this the story of Zacchaeus? Scrooge? Can you think of any other story of stealing redeemed?

Why do you think Judas's stealing (John 12:6) was not redeemed?

Wrap Up (5 minutes)

Share your prayer requests with one another.

Confirm the date and location of the next meeting.

Close by reading out loud the following prayer.

Dear God,

"The earth is Yours and the fullness thereof." We enter it with nothing, and it is sure that we will leave with nothing. It is all Yours, Lord. To think that we can ever truly possess anything is an illusion at best. So, Lord, help us to handle the things of this world lightly, knowing that everything that would tempt us to steal will eventually fall away to nothing. The only thing that truly lasts is love, and love cannot be stolen. It can only be given as a gift, and received as a grace. So, Lord, we ask to receive that which You want to give—Your love, Your mercy, and Your life! Forgive us of all our vain striving and stealing. Help us to focus on the one and only thing that makes sense to possess—heaven. Amen.

Command Nine:
The Truth, the Whole Truth, and Nothing but the Truth, So Help Me God!

Americans once took the witness stand in a courtroom, raised their right hands, placed their left hands on the Bible, and repeated the oath, "I swear to tell the truth, the whole truth, and nothing but the truth, *so help me God.*" Taking this oath presumed two things.

First—"the truth" was hard to pin down.

Second—getting at "the truth" required God's help.

This courtroom practice held steady for generations, but now you can lay your hand on the Bible if you like, or the Koran, the U.S. Constitution, Walt Whitman's *Leaves of Grass,* or nothing at all. You can swear by God, Allah, the Republican party, the Democratic National Committee, or your own personal higher power. Truth in the American courtroom is no longer grounded on anything higher than our own human capacity to tell it.

But here's the question—just how good are men and women at telling the truth? Day-to-day experience suggests not very good at all. People regularly exaggerate and manipulatethe truth. How many times has someone said to you things like, "Your secret is safe with me," only to discover it just wasn't true.

Remember the iconic scene in the movie *A Few Good Men.* LTJG Daniel Kaffee (Tom Cruise) cross-examines Colonel Nathan Jessep (Jack Nicholson) on the witness stand. Cruise as the naval defense lawyer gets in the face of his witness, Nicholson, and demands, "I want the truth!" To which Nicholson roars, "You can't handle the truth!" The scene burned itself upon the American psyche because we all knew it was right on—we can't handle the truth. Experience confirms what the Bible warns—that the human heart is corrupt and cannot be trusted for the truth. The Scripture cautions:

> The heart is deceitful above all things.
>
> *Jeremiah* 17:9

You've heard people blurt out things like, "I swear on a stack of Bibles!" or "The Lord strike me dead if I'm not telling you the truth!" Such expressions testify that we all instinctively know we need help with the truth—that our word alone is not good enough. That we need divine assistance!

America's founders certainly believed this simple wisdom. Enlightened thinkers like John Adams and James Madison were convinced that the human heart was untrustworthy, which is why they built the American government upon a system of accountability with checks and balances. The founders knew that no one individual or branch of government could be trusted for the truth.

Today, public skepticism prevails. America's rank and file assume that politicians, financiers, journalists, Hollywood—anyone—will all spin the truth to their own advantage. Major stories involving the media highlight just how bold some can get with their lies. Remember the "autobiography" of James Fry, *A Million*

Little Pieces? It was a runaway bestseller because Oprah Winfrey recommended it to her book club. But it came to light that Fry fabricated large sections of his story and was forced to endure the humiliation of being scolded by Oprah on national television ("I feel you have betrayed millions of readers."). James Fry is only one example. There are others. Stephen Glass a reporter for the *New Republic,* Jayson Blair a reporter for the *New York Times,* and Janet Cooke a Pulitzer Prize winner from the *Washington Post* each lied in the articles they wrote only to be publically humiliated. Such stories underscore the age-old wisdom, "Don't believe everything you read." Just because it's written in the *New York Times* or the *National Review* doesn't make it true.

And there is a new wrinkle to truthfulness which poses a baffling challenge. It is this: many Americans no longer believe that "the truth" even exists. According to a 2004 survey conducted by pollster George Barna only 35 percent of Americans actually believe in an absolute/universal truth.[6] And why is this such a problem? Because the American courtroom depends on citizen juries, and if these citizen juries no longer believe "the truth" even exists, then how are they to judge between right or wrong, good or bad, true or false? By what standard are they to evaluate the truth? Popular opinion? But isn't popular opinion easy prey for manipulation? You bet it is!

Another reason the loss of faith in the truth is such a problem is because lying has become so pervasive throughout America. Comedian Jim Carrey starred in a 1999 movie entitled Liar Liar. The plot involved a two-faced money-grabbing lawyer who woke up one morning unable to lie, and how the truth provoked pandemonium in his life and in the lives of everyone around him. What interested me about this film was how no movie critic protested the movie's basic premise—that people are liars. Not even the nation's lawyers, whom the movie savaged, raised an objection. Evidently lying is generally agreed to be normative. In fact, USA Today described lying as "America's pastime."[7] The article's first line stated: "EVERYBODY LIES. From the president of the U.S. to Congress to the smallest citizen in the country, we are a nation of liars." From birth we possess an instinctive compulsion to distort the truth. Students cheat. Businesspeople fudge facts. The news media spins. Preachers exaggerate. Job applicants pad their resumes.

Remember the crazy story of Coach George O'Leary? In 2001 Coach O'Leary was hired as the head football coach for none other than Notre Dame University, the most prestigious of all college coaching positions. But a mere five days after he was hired the university demanded his resignation. Why? Because of "inconsistencies" on his résumé. He cited a master's degree that he hadn't earned. And in the height of irony, he claimed to have earned a varsity letter in football while an undergraduate at the University of New Hampshire, but there was no record of him ever having played. He never even played! In his statement to the press, Coach O'Leary blamed the inaccuracies on "résumé padding." It's claimed that 50–80 percent of all resumes can easily be classified as misleading, and that 70 percent of America's college students are willing to lie on their résumés to get a job.[8]

So ingrained is lying within our culture that Doug Mushro wrote an amusing article entitled "Great American Lies." In it he shares America's top ten fibs:

10. I'll start my diet tomorrow.
9. Money cheerfully refunded…
8. Give me your number, and the doctor will call you right back.
7. One size fits all.
6. This will hurt me more than it will hurt you.
5. It's not the money, it's the principle.
4. I just need a minute of your time.
3. This offer is limited to the first 100 people.

2. We service what we sell.
1. The check is in the mail.

You may laugh, but these familiar phrases reveal just how deeply lies are embedded into the core of our culture.

The unvarnished truth is that you and I are liars—prone to exaggerate, to omit certain facts, to tell half truths, to twist and distort facts, and invent falsehoods. Human nature is not to be trusted, which is why America's founders had courtroom witnesses place their hands on the Bible to ask God for help. They did so because of what the Ninth Commandment says:

> You shall not bear false witness against your neighbor.
>
> *Exodus* 20:16 (NRSV)

The Ninth Commandment's original focus was with telling the truth in court. But Scripture as a whole makes it clear that this commandment involves more than just the courtroom. Indeed, the Living Bible goes so far as to expand the commandment to say:

> You must not lie.
>
> *Exodus* 20:16 (LB)

The positive way to express this command is to simply say— "be honest." Live a life of integrity by telling the truth at every turn.

> It is better to be poor but honest, than to be a lying fool.
>
> *Proverbs* 19:1 (GN)

Unfortunately, lying today is not considered a big deal. It's frowned upon, and in some instances its technically illegal, but the prevailing attitude is that "everyone does it." But lying is a big deal to God—a very big deal! According to the Scriptures there are seven things that God hates. "Hate" is a strong word. Scripture does not employ it casually, so you might want to sit up and take notice. The seven things that God hates are:

> ...haughtiness, *lying,* murdering, plotting evil, eagerness to do wrong, *a false witness,* sowing discord among brothers.
>
> *Proverbs* 6:16–19 (LB)

Note that two of God's seven hatreds involve distorting the truth. Clearly, it's a big deal for God. We may excuse ourselves for telling "little white lies," but evidently God is not as casual with the truth.

In 1978 M. Scott Peck published a smash hit book entitled *The Road Less Traveled* that helped millions of readers to understand the link between love and truth. It sold seven million copies, and was on the *NY Times* bestseller list for years. I personally read the book three times. It changed my life. Five years later in 1983, Dr. Peck published a second book entitled *People of the Lie.* In this chilling book, he studied evil and its relationship to lying. He concluded that the surest way to identify the presence of evil is to look for the lie, because evil always betrays itself with lies. It's the only language evil knows. This is no surprise because Jesus Himself declared Satan to be the "father of lies." To lie is to speak the devil's own language. It is, therefore, no wonder why God is so firmly set against it. The Scripture says,

> ...all liars—their doom is in the Lake that burns with fire and sulfur ...the second death.
>
> *Revelation* 21:8 (LB)

Let me caution here that not all lies are damnable and not all truth is appropriate. For example, during World War II, as the Nazis searched for Jews, sometimes it was necessary to lie to protect the innocent. Surely, telling the truth is the ideal in a perfect world, but ours is not a perfect world. Sometimes the truth can endanger the innocent. The Bible tells us that when King David, his men, and their families, lived among the Philistines, he lied about his loyalties. He did this to ensure the safety of his people.

But the broad principle of the Ninth Commandment directs us to commit ourselves to the truth. Yet the problem is we just can't do it! We are born liars. So let's take a look at some of the specifics of the Ninth Commandment, and attempt to answer three basic questions:

How do we lie?
Why do we lie?
And what's the cure?

How Do We Lie?

We have a certain genius for lying: we exaggerate, omit details, distort facts, and we out and out invent falsehoods. But there are two particular types of lying that most of us employ: half truths and denial.

The first lie recorded in the Bible is a half truth. It is spoken in the garden of Eden by the serpent. The serpent asks Eve, "Did God say, 'You shall not eat of any tree of the garden'?"

Eve replies, "We may eat anything except the forbidden fruit, lest we die."

And this is where the first lie is told, for the serpent claims, "You will not die."

This statement is technically true, but only half true. When Adam and Eve ate the forbidden fruit, they did not immediately die, but the trust that existed between themselves and God certainly did.

Half truths are the most common form of lying, and the most effective. A half truth disguises a lie. Like the time I had dinner with Hall of Fame NFL quarterback Dan Marino in Miami. It sounds impressive, but only because I fail to mention that it was at a fundraising banquet with three hundred other people and that he was at the head table while I was in the cheap seats. For me to claim that I had dinner with Dan Marino is using the truth to deceive. It's a lie.

Families employ half truths all the time. Husbands tell wives they are busy working late; when they are really avoiding the challenges at home. Wives tell husbands they don't feel well when they are really avoiding their husbands. And teenagers tell parents they are staying with a friend when they are really just meeting there with the plan to go out later.

The half truth has become an art form for the advertisers who hype the truth, the politicians who spin the truth, the lawyers who shade the truth, and loved ones who sugarcoat the truth. It is all an attempt to manipulate. But to followers of Jesus the Scripture has this to say,

> No more lying, then! Everyone must tell the truth to his brother, because we are all members together in the body of Christ.
>
> *Ephesians* 4:25 *(*GN*)*

The Ninth Commandment directs believers to speak the truth, the whole truth, and nothing but the truth, so help us God. Everyone has trouble telling the truth—especially half truths, and it is for this reason that God directs us to seek His divine assistance. He understands that we have trouble with the truth, but we must be willing to approach the truth on His terms, not our own.

Another destructive form of lying is denial. Alcoholics deny ruining their lives with drinking. Workaholics deny ruining their family lives with over work. Husbands and wives deny ruining their marriages with pornography. It's typical for the addictive personality to say things like, "I can stop drinking/smoking/doping anytime I want," but the cold hard facts are that their life is out of control. There used to be a bumper sticker that read, "Reality bites." This is exactly why denial is popular. Reality can feel too tough to take, and some cope by denying it. Earlier I mentioned disgraced journalist Stephan Blair. Rather than accept personal responsibility for his plagiarism, Blair blamed his lying on a battle with bipolar disorder and drug problems. In other words—he wouldn't take personal responsibility—he denied it. So too did President Bush deny the mistakes that led to the invasion of Iraq, and President Clinton deny he had sexual relations with that woman, Miss Lewinsky. Denial is the ego's first line of defense. Whenever the ego is threatened, the kneejerk reaction is to deny, deny, deny. But to deny the truth doesn't make the truth go away. Sooner or later the hard realities of the truth will bite. If you don't pay your rent, you may convince yourself that nothing bad is going to happen, and indeed nothing bad does happen for months. But eventually there comes the day when the sheriff knocks on the door and escorts you from what was your residence. Denial is simple—first and foremost, it is when you lie to yourself!

Breaking free of denial is not something done alone. The human instinct to lie is just too quick and clever. The denial is out of the mouth before any clear thinking is done. What is needed is at least one other person with whom you are willing to sit down and take the time to be 100 percent transparent and accountable. Without this accountability, the lie will prevail. There isn't a person alive who doesn't resist confessing sin, and yet confession is the first step toward the truth. After all the Scripture says,

> If we say we have no sin (denial), we deceive ourselves, and the truth is not in us.
>
> 1 *John* 1:8 *(*RSV*)*

Mercifully, this very same scripture goes on to reassure us:

> If we confess our sins (the Lord) is faithful and just, and will forgive our sins and cleanse us from all unrighteousness.
>
> 1 *John* 1:9

You are not alone in having trouble with the truth. But God wants more than to just comfort you with the assurance that you "are only human." God wants you to have a heart for the truth and a life full of integrity.

So Why Do We Lie?

Obviously we lie because we assume it's to our advantage. We lie to protect our self interests. We lie because we are angry and want revenge. We lie because we are proud and want to impress others. The biggest reason we lie is because we're afraid the truth will hurt us. Let me say this again because it merits repeating. We fear the truth will hurt us! Fear is at the root of most lies. Indeed, there are a thousand and one different reasons why we lie, but it all boils down to the fact that the truth does not live in us.

> The truth is not in us.
>
> 1 *John* 1:8

Truth must be born sometime after our physical birth. The Bible is clear that we are all to be born a second time, born to God's Spirit, which is the Spirit of Truth. Jesus once promised His disciples,

> I will ask the Father, and He will give you another Helper, the Spirit of truth…
>
> *John* 14:16–17 *(*GN*)*

Until the Spirit of Truth is born in us, we will resort to lies anytime our fears get the best of us, which leads to the last question.

What Is the Cure?

Ironically, honesty starts with accepting your own dishonesty. Most everyone has an excuse, an explanation, or a rationalization for his or her duplicity. Rare is the person who quickly takes personal responsibility for his or her lies. But the first and most essential step toward integrity is to confess your lying nature. In other words, the first step in the cure for lying is to get honest with your dishonesty.

But getting honest with dishonesty is not easy. Many years of ministry inform me that people will do just about anything to avoid coming to terms with their own duplicity. But for those who take courage and confess, the door to the truth swings wide open.

The second step in the cure is to stay close to the truth. Naturally debate rages as to just what the truth is. But this is where the Christian faith shines, for Christianity maintains that the Truth is both clear and approachable—not at all abstract. It is neither a fact, an opinion, nor a philosophy. For the Christian believer the truth is a person ...the person of Jesus Christ. The world has sought the truth in science, philosophy, religion, and law. Through the ages different things were presumed to be true: that the world is flat and at the center of the universe, the atom is the smallest particle in creation, technology would save us. Such "truths" were assumed uncontestable at one time in history, but now they are all passé. However the claim of the New Testament is that all truth is embodied in Jesus, and for this reason believers can stay close to the truth, not because of their sparkling intelligence, high moral character, spiritual wisdom, or philosophic sophistication. No. They can stay close to the truth because they trust Jesus to stay close to them.

The implication for this gospel is profound! No longer are we forced to find the truth. The Christian gospel proclaims that the truth in Jesus Christ is looking harder for us than we are for it. The mission of Jesus has always been simple:

> ...to seek and to save the lost.
>
> *Luke* 19:10 (RSV)

Jesus of Nazareth, the very embodiment of truth, seeks to find us so that we might receive the truth, the whole truth, and nothing but the truth. And just how can this truth be expressed? In this way:

> We are great sinners, and He is a great savior!

We are great sinners to be sure. History confirms our shameless self-centeredness and unspeakable horrors. We are obsessed with the "I," "me," "my" of our lives and indifferent to others. This truth is unassailable and reverberates throughout the human chronicle. Fortunately, it is only half of the above equation. For as wicked as we can be, the splendor of God's grace is that much more heartening, for it has the power to rescue liars and cheats such as you and me, and transform us into men and women of integrity! Alexander Pope once wrote that "an honest man was God's greatest work." You see, integrity is not the norm; it is a divine achievement. Honestly is what God's Spirit brings to birth inside the hearts of men and women who have the courage to admit and confess their lying nature.

This is just what happened in the life of the Apostle Peter. Peter was a liar. He lied when he claimed he would follow Jesus all the way to His death, and that same night he lied again when he denied Jesus three times in His moment of truth. A liar like Peter hardly seemed to be the best candidate for leading the earliest Christian church. But God's Spirit of truth transformed Peter. He was changed from the inside out. Peter the liar was transformed into Peter the rock, the first and greatest leader of the earliest church.

Conclusion

A fairy tale's innocence can make it easier to accept a difficult truth that we might otherwise resist. One such truth is our penchant for lying, and the fairy tale that helps us accept it is Walt Disney's Oscar-winning (1940) production, *Pinocchio.*

Pinocchio, you will remember, is the tale of a little wooden puppet brought to life by the deep magic of the Blue Fairy. Pinocchio was sweet and winsome, but he had one flaw that nearly ruined him and everyone around him. He had no conscience; and because he had no conscience, he wasn't able to tell the truth. And every time he lied, his little wooden nose would grow. It didn't take long for Pinocchio's nose to grow so long from the tall tales he told that it extended several feet beyond his face, and sprouted branches, leaves, and even a bird's nest. Naturally, he was horrified and begged the Blue Fairy to restore his nose. It was then that the Blue Fairy shared this wisdom. She said, "Pinocchio, a lie keeps growing and growing until it becomes as plain as the nose on your face." Amen!

No doubt some of your own lies have grown and grown 'til they became as "plain as the nose on your face." But just as the Blue Fairy restored Pinocchio's nose, so too can the power of Christ restore you. This is not to say that the Lord will magically make all your lies go away. He won't. Indeed, you may have to suffer the consequences of the lies you've told. The Lord will forgive you, but that doesn't mean that the world will excuse you. Neither will the Lord stop you from lying again. You're free to do as you choose. You see, the Lord's focus is not on your lies, but on His truth! The Lord is committed to empowering you with the truth, the whole truth, and nothing but the truth! The Lord doesn't help you with your lies; He helps you with His truth.

You and I weren't born with the truth, and we certainly don't grow into it naturally. Quite the opposite. We are born liars, and until we admit our lying, it remains our language. But the good news of the gospel is that the Lord was willing to take extreme measures to give us the truth. He allowed the lies of friends and foes alike to nail Him to a cross that all might see just as plain as the noses on their faces the most profound truth of all. That...

We are great sinners, and He is a great savior!

Study Guide:
The Truth, the Whole Truth, and Nothing but the Truth, So Help Me God!

90 minutes

Introduction (5 minutes)

Briefly

Create amongst yourselves a courtroom scene. Act out the swearing in of a witness who is about to give testimony. What words are used for the swearing in? Will the left hand be placed on the Bible? Discuss why.

Opening Discussion/Warm Up(20 minutes)

Vote amongst yourselves which of the following is the most annoying lie. What about it makes it so annoying?

10. I'll start my diet tomorrow.
9. Money cheerfully refunded...

8. Give me your number, and the doctor will call you right back.
7. One size fits all.
6. This will hurt me more than it will hurt you.
5. It's not the money, it's the principle.
4. I just need a minute of your time.
3. This offer is limited to the first 100 people.
2. We service what we sell.
1. The check is in the mail.

How good are men and women at telling the truth? Are children any better? Give illustrations.

The "founding fathers" of American government (John Adams, Alexander Hamilton, and James Madison) created a system of "checks and balances." Why? Based on the system of government they created, did the founders have much confidence that individuals and/or institutions without oversight could be trusted for the truth?

George Barna's research reveals that only 35 percent of Americans actually believe in an "absolute/universal truth." Most Americans believe that truth is relative ...dependent upon circumstances. Why is this a problem for the American judicial system?

Is Lying a Big Deal?(15 *minutes)*

Divide the room in two and ask participants to go to one end if they think people consider telling a lie a big deal, or the other end if they don't.

Reassemble and read the following Scriptures out loud together:

> There are six things the Lord hates, seven that are detestable to Him: haughty eyes, a lying tongue, hands that shed innocent blood, a heart that devises wicked schemes, feet that are quick to rush into evil, a false witness who pours out lies, and a man who stirs up dissension among brothers.
>
> *Proverbs* 6:16–17

Based on the above, does God consider lying a big deal? Consider the following scripture:

> ...all liars—their doom is in the Lake that burns with fire and sulfur ...the second death.
>
> *Revelation* 21:8 (LB)

How Do We Lie?(15 minutes)

What is a half truth?

Read the following statement together:

> Families speak half-truths all the time. Husbands tell wives they are busy working late; when they are really avoiding the challenges at home. Wives tell husbands they don't feel well when they are really avoiding their husbands. And teenagers tell parents they are staying with a friend when they are really just meeting there with the plan to go out later. The half truth has become an art form for the advertisers who hype the truth, the politicians who spin the truth, the lawyers who shade the truth, and loved ones who sugarcoat the truth.

Can you share an example of a half-truth used in your family? What makes half-truths so effective as lies?

What is denial? Can you think of a famous example of someone who denied his or her moral failure?

Does personal intelligence make one more or less likely to employ denial, or does it just make the denial more complicated?

Read out loud the following scripture:

> If we claim to be without sin, we deceive ourselves, and the truth is not in us. If we confess our sins, God is faithful and just and will forgive…
>
> 1 *John* 1:8

According to the above scripture, what is the way out?

Why Do We Lie?(5 minutes)

The Bible offers the simplest and most precise explanation for why we lie.

> The truth is not in us.
>
> 1 *John* 1:8

From where does the truth come?

> I will ask the Father, and He will give you another Helper, the Spirit of truth...
>
> *John* 14:16–17 *(*GN*)*

According to the Scripture, are we born with an instinct for telling the truth?

What Is the Cure?(15 *minutes)*

According to scripture, how does Jesus describe Himself?

> I am the way, and the *truth,* and the life.
>
> *John* 14:6

What does it mean for Jesus to be "the truth"? Read together Colossians 1:15–20.

If Jesus is "the truth," what is the best way to stay close to the truth?

If we feel incapable of staying close to Christ does Jesus promise to abandon us, forsake us, or seek us out? Does the truth seek us out ...even when we are not open to the truth?

> I have come to seek and to save the lost.
>
> *Luke* 19:10 *(*RSV*)*

What is the truest thing you know? Did you select this truth, or did this truth select you?

Name a liar in scripture who was transformed by the Spirit of God into a woman or man of integrity.

Conclusion(10 minutes)

Have someone retell the fairytale of Pinocchio and what happened to Pinocchio when he told a lie. When caught lying, the Blue Fairy said to Pinocchio,

> Pinocchio, a lie keeps growing and growing until it becomes as plain as the nose on your face.

Is this true only in fairy tales, or is this true?

What is true about the following statement?

We are great sinners, but the lord is a great savior!

Wrap Up (5 minutes)

Share your prayer requests with one another.

Confirm the date and location of the next meeting.

Close by reading out loud the following prayer.

Dear God,

The truth is hard to tell. We tend to exaggerate, deny, or just make it up. Indeed, sometimes we are tempted to deny that the truth even exists. But You have made the truth clear and approachable—not at all abstract. You are the truth, Lord! You are at the center of all that is true. All truth eventually leads to You. And when we find ourselves unable to hold on to the truth, we trust, Lord, that You will hold on to us. The truth will always prevail in our lives, not because of our integrity, but because of Yours. Lord, help us to receive You that Your truth might guide our steps. In Your name we pray. Amen.

Command Ten:
The Most Dangerous Word in English

My two-year-old daughter just learned the most dangerous word in the English language. It is a four-letter word, but it's not the "f-word." The f-bomb may be rude and crude, but it is mostly harmless compared to the word my daughter discovered. The word my daughter learned is the little four-letter word "mine."

"My baby doll ...mine."

"My toy ...mine."

Since my daughter learned this four-letter word there's been less peace in the Green household. Regular explosions occur when she grabs her older sister's doll and runs away squealing, "Mine, mine..." only to have her older sister shriek like a wounded animal in outrage. They race through the house screaming claims and counterclaims of ownership. They tussle on the couch. They pinch, they scratch, they pull hair, they scream! The fighting escalates until their mother or I intervene to untangle their different claims of property rights.

Raising three children, I'm learning that the problem of possession is not about the sparkle and allure of any one particular toy. The problem is deeper—almost genetic—for it's nothing parents teach. They don't have to. Children are infected with it from birth. The problem is rooted in an all too human self-centeredness, one that inevitably breeds the green-eyed monster of envy. And envy is always accompanied by its wicked cousins: jealousy, resentment, and strife. As the Scripture declares,

> ...you covet and cannot obtain; so you fight...
>
> *James* 4:2 (ESV)

Story after story is told in the Bible of those who covet what someone else has, and such stories never end well. David coveted Uriah's wife, Bathsheba, which only led to deceit and death. Prince Absalom coveted his father David's throne, which only led to deceit and death. King Ahab and Queen Jezebel coveted the vineyard of Naboth, and it only led to deceit and death. The scribes and Pharisees coveted Jesus's popularity, and it only led to deceit and death. Such stories confirm that sin isn't so much about what we do; it's who we are! Our desire to acquire is instinctive, it is born in us. My daughter may just now be learning how to speak, but her desire to acquire was hard wired into her. It is as natural to her as hunger and thirst. What's worse, her desire to acquire inevitably mutates into the ugly urge to envy her older sister and friends, to covet their things, and to fight for more.

In the New Testament, I know of only one instance where someone turned down an invitation to follow Jesus. It was the rich young man who fell before Jesus, asking, "Good teacher, what must I do to inherit eternal life?"

Jesus responded by asking, "Have you kept the commandments, do not kill, do not commit adultery, do not steal, do not lie, do not defraud, honor your father and mother?"

"Yes, Lord," the young man answered, "all these I have kept from my youth."

Jesus looked at the young man, loved him, and extended an invitation. "You lack one thing," Jesus said to him, "go and sell all that you have, give to the poor, and you will have treasure in heaven; and come, follow me."

The rich young man, however, turned down Jesus' invitation, because "Great were his possessions." Evidently, when given a choice between Jesus and his possessions, the rich young man chose his possessions. After the rich young man walked away, Jesus had this to say,

> How hard it will be for those who have riches to enter the kingdom of God! It is easier for a camel to go through the eye of a needle than for a rich man to enter the kingdom of God.
>
> *Mark* 10:23, 25 *(*RSV*)*

Our slavery to "stuff," especially other people's stuff, is a curse that drives too many of us to perpetual unhappiness. To covet is to be a slave to what is not "mine." It inspires cruel comparisons that poison relationships with a cancerous envy. It is a curse that drives many to perpetual discontent. But within the Tenth Commandment lies the secret to real contentment in life, so let's take a closer look.

A Feeling Condemned

The Tenth Commandment is different from the first nine. Commands one through nine are centered on actions, but the Tenth Commandment centers on a feeling - the desire to acquire - the out of control urge that mutates healthy wants into unhealthy envy.

Just how concerned is God with our desire to acquire? Well, consider this. Out of the entire spectrum of human emotions, passions, and feelings, it is the one and only feeling God specifically regulates with His Ten Commandments. He says,

> You shall not covet your neighbor's house; you shall not covet your neighbor's wife, or his manservant, or his maidservant, or his ox, or his ass, or anything that is your neighbor's.
>
> *Exodus* 20:17

Jesus, by the way, echoed this standard when He said,

> Take heed, and beware of all covetousness; for a man's life does not consist in the abundance of his possessions.
>
> *Luke* 12:15 *(*RSV*)*

Again, the Tenth Commandment does not prohibit any specific action. Instead it focuses on an interior attitude—what some call the attitude of ingratitude.

Yet how can God outlaw a feeling? How can God condemn me for being piggish with a sudden impulse of envy? But this is exactly what the Tenth Commandment outlaws. Evidently, God does not consider such feelings to be involuntary. With the Tenth Commandment God declares a resolute "no" to the overweening urge to possess whatever is not "mine."

By the way, covetousness is a disease that afflicts us all, rich and poor alike. All are vulnerable. A rich man can covet something a poor man has just as surely as a poor man can covet something a rich man has. After all,

> The poor man would give his soul,
> If only he had the rich man's gold;
> The rich man would give all his wealth,
> If only he had the poor man's health.[9]

Saying "No" to Oneself

To put your finger squarely on the meaning of the Tenth Commandment is elusive. After all, it condemns a feeling, and feelings don't always come into sharp focus, especially when you don't like to admit them. I've been a pastor for twenty-six years, and I can't recall anyone ever confessing to me their sin of covetousness. I've had people confess murders, thefts, and adulteries, but I've yet to have someone tell me they've secretly envied their neighbor's new car, yet it happens all the time. Indeed, the Tenth Commandment may be the command most frequently broken, but it is also the sin most resolutely denied.

The Tenth Commandment cautions that to covet our neighbor's things is lethal …*even if we don't act on the urge!* The desire alone is enough to ruin our lives with perpetual dissatisfaction! As the Scripture warns:

> Whoever loves money never has money enough;
> Whoever loves wealth is never satisfied…
>
> *Ecclesiastes* 5:10

God's Tenth Commandment warns that this urge, this greed, this desire to acquire is cursed because it can never be fully satisfied. It simply leads to an existence of perpetual dissatisfaction and brokenness—to deceit and death.

I worked with students at Princeton University who tend to ask a lot of questions. Once I was stopped short by a question that tied me in knots. The question was this: "Just what is maturity?" I hemmed and hawed in an effort to respond, but I wasn't able to zero in on a satisfying answer. But I think I have one now. Maturity is this: a capacity to say "no" to oneself. This is largely what the Tenth Commandment is all about. It helps us discern when to say "no" to ourselves. When our wants tempt us to pursue something or someone that belongs to someone else, we are to say "no" to ourselves.

The Tenth Commandment is a negative statement— "Thou shalt not…" But it can also be stated positively: "Desire the right things for the right reasons." The Christian life is not about rising above all desires—that's Buddhism. Buddhism maintains that life's greatest problem is suffering and that all suffering springs from our desires. Simply let go of all desire and suffering is released. But Christianity believes just the opposite. It believes that humanity's greatest problem is sin, and that the way to overcome it is to focus our desire for God. After all, the Bible affirms that:

> Desire fulfilled is a tree of life.
>
> *Proverbs* 13:12

Desire is considered a good thing by the Christian faith. After all, God gave us all our desires, and God intends to help us fulfill them. The Scripture affirms:

> Delight yourself in the Lord, and He will give you the desires of your heart.
>
> *Psalm* 37:4

Again, desire is considered positive by God. Desire is the steam that drives the human engine, so it is good. After all, without desire there would be no charity, no service, and above all no love!

But it is also true that desires can get the better of you and me and overwhelm us. We are easily confounded by our many wants, and the danger is that our desires will eventually own us much more profoundly than we will ever own them. This is the trap for which the Tenth Commandment serves as a caution.

In Thomas Jefferson's first draft of the Declaration of Independence, he wrote that all people had the inalienable rights to "life, liberty, and the pursuit of property." The committee that reviewed Jefferson's first draft, however, changed his original wording from "the pursuit of property" to "the pursuit of happiness." But for Americans today, it's all pretty much the same thing. Happiness is all tied up in property and possessions. Many freely subscribe to the philosophy that the one who dies with the most toys wins. But I've stood at the side of many death beds, and I have yet to hear anyone scream for more "stuff" as they gulp down their last breaths. I've witnessed dying men and women give away their things, but I've never seen anyone at death's door pleading for more stuff. The Tenth Commandment is God's Declaration of Independence from the tyranny of our many wants. God wants us to be free from any desire that would enslave us ...especially our desire to acquire ...our need for the things of the world to be "mine."

The Blessings of Others!

Commandment Ten puts a simple question before us: "Will we rely upon God to satisfy our desires, or will we grasp after the things of others?" It forces a decision—whether or not to trust God. The Scripture proclaims that God's capacity to supply your needs and satisfy your desires is unlimited. It says:

> Delight yourself in the Lord, and He will give you the desires of your heart.
>
> *Psalm* 37:4

Notice, the Scripture says that God "will" give you the desires of your heart. It doesn't say that He might or that He could or that He will think about it if you're good enough. His desire to fulfill you is far beyond anything you can ask or imagine. Again, the Scripture promises,

> ...God will meet all your needs according to his glorious riches in Christ Jesus.
>
> *Philippians* 4:19

But this is not to say that God gives equally. God is gracious, but He blesses some with more of the world's things than others, and those who receive less must choose their response—whether or not to envy the blessings of others!

Jesus once told this story about the inequity of God's blessing.

> There was once a farmer who early in the morning went to town to hire laborers. After agreeing upon a price for a day's work, he hired some of the men. Later that same morning he returned to town and hired more laborers. Again at noon the farmer returned to town and hired still more workers, and again at three, and again at five. At six o'clock the farmer rang the bell for work to stop, and he gathered his workers to pay them. But what he did was a shock, for he paid everybody the same wage. Those who had started early in the morning complained, resenting the good fortune of those who were hired late in the afternoon. But the farmer responded, "Did I not pay you what we had agreed? And is it not my money ...can't I be generous with it as I choose?"
>
> *Matthew* 20:1–16

God promises to give what we need, but sometimes He gives more to others! He is not always equitable with His blessings, and we must decide how to respond—with envy or praise.

Dr. James W. Moor, a Methodist pastor in Houston, wrote a book entitled *You Can Get Bitter or Better.* In it he identifies three levels of love. The first is the easiest; it is to love those who love you. The second is more difficult; it is to love those who don't love you. The third level of love is the most difficult and reserved for the saints; it is to love those who are more fortunate and successful than you. Like I said, this is the love of the saints—to love those who enjoy more of life's blessing than you—without envy.

Just Passing Through!

It is predictable to hear that envy stems from wanting too much …that our desires are too greedy for our own good. But the Bible illustrates that the reverse is true. Consider for a moment what we covet. Money, cars, houses, clothes, power, position, and pleasure. Ponder this—none of these will exist on the other side of death! Beyond the grave, who will care whether we drove a Lexus, a Lincoln, or a lemon?

The problem with our coveting is not that we desire too much but that we desire too little. We spend our lives envious of the passing things of this world …money, cars, success, all while God reaches out to us with the riches of heaven. The Christian solution to envy and covetousness is not to throw water over the fires of our desire, but to intensify them. Indeed, the more we covet the best things, the things of heaven, the less we will covet the passing things of this life. After all, the Scripture counsels us to:

> …desire the greater gifts.
>
> 1 *Corinthians* 12:31

In the end, what is most meaningful is not what is "mine" but what is "Thine!" After all, we are just passing through. We don't even fully own the bodies we inhabit. They betray us, and in the end, we will lay them down. Not even our memories are our own for these too will be surrendered at the appointed time. In the end there is nothing that is "mine" forever. It is all His—the One who created it all. And the question that truly matters is not one of mine but Thine …*Am I wholly Thine, Lord?*

Among all the stories in ancient monastic folklore, one stands out as a particularly insightful commentary on the Tenth Commandment.

> A disciple traveled for miles to sit at the feet of an old nun who had acquired an unusual reputation for holiness.

> People came from far and wide simply to watch her work, to listen to her chant, to hear her comment on the Scriptures. Here without doubt was a person of substance, an impacting personality, and imposing spiritual giant.
>
> But what the seeker actually found when he finally reached the site of her hermitage, however, was only a tiny little woman sitting on the floor of a bare room plaiting straw baskets alone. Shocked, the seeker said, "Old woman, where are your books? Where are your chair and footstool? Where are your bed and mattress?"
>
> And the old woman answered him back, "And where are yours?"
>
> "But I'm only passing through," The seeker said.
>
> "And so am I," said the old woman knowingly. "So am I."[10]

My two-year-old girl has learned the most dangerous word in the English language—the little four-letter word "mine." As her father, it is my calling to do everything I can to teach and inspire a different word for her to live up to— "Thine." Why? Because, she too is just passing through.

What God Covets

I close with a last bit of good news.

If you are guilty of covetousness, keep in mind that God is also guilty. You see, God covets something that is someone else's possession. Let me explain in a roundabout way.

At birth you and I are citizens of this world, and the Bible is absolutely clear that the true king of this world is the devil himself. Here's chapter and verse:

> ...The whole world is under the control of the evil one.
>
> 1 *John* 5:19

The New Testament refers to Satan as:

> the prince of this world.
>
> *John* 16:11

> god of this world.
>
> 2 *Corinthians* 4:4 (GN)

We don't require Scripture to confirm this. Just glance at the front page of the morning paper. The headlines are enough to confirm who's in charge. But even if we are citizens of the world, and so subjects of the evil one, nonetheless, God covets us. We may be born the devil's possession, but God has the desire to acquire each and every one of us. This is what salvation is all about …it is a rescue operation. St. Paul put it this way,

> For (the Lord) has rescued us from the dominion of darkness and brought us into the Kingdom of the Son He loves.
>
> *Colossians* 1:13

Yes, God covets the possession of the devil—He covets you and me. He covets us, not because we are bright and shiny, not because of the luster of our character and spiritual maturity. He covets us because we bear His image. When He looks at us, the first word that comes to Him is "mine"!

Study Guide: the Most Dangerous Word in English

90 minutes

Introduction (10 minutes)

Briefly

Individually select the word believed to be the most dangerous word in English and why? Have each participant share the word they've chosen and why.

Opening Discussion/Warm Up(15 minutes)

In the New Testament there is one story of an individual who is invited by Jesus to follow Him, but who refuses. Read together Mark 10:17–31 and answer the following questions.

- If the rich young man was satisfied with his wealth, would he have sought out Jesus in the first place?
- What specifically does the rich young man want?
- Does Jesus reject the young man, or does He extend an invitation?
- What prevents the young man from accepting Jesus's invitation?
- What is Jesus's response to the young man's refusal?
- What is the logical application of this story in your life when it comes to the things we covet?

A Feeling Condemned(15 minutes)

Does the Tenth Commandment condemn any specific action? Or does it condemn a feeling?

> You shall not covet your neighbor's house; you shall not covet your neighbor's wife, or his manservant, or his

> maidservant, or his ox, or his ass, or anything that is your neighbor's.
>
> *Exodus* 20:17

If God can condemn a feeling, does it suggest that we have at least some control over such feelings?

How much control do you currently have over your covetousness?

Saying "No" to Oneself (15 minutes)

Define amongst yourselves what it means to be emotionally mature.

Does being able to say "no" to yourself have anything to do with emotional maturity?

What relationship does saying "no" to oneself have with the Tenth Commandment?

Restate the Tenth Commandment positively.

Buddhism's counsel is to strip oneself of all human desire, whereas Christianity directs its followers to focus and intensify one's desire onto Christ. Which is the more realistic approach—eliminating desire or refocusing it?

Discuss amongst yourselves the following two verses of scripture. What are they trying to communicate to you?

> Desire fulfilled is a tree of life.
>
> *Proverbs* 13:12

> Delight yourself in the Lord, and He will give you the desires of your heart.
>
> *Psalm* 37:4

The Blessings of Others (10 minutes)

Is God "fair" in the way He blesses different people?

Can God's blessing of others provoke envy? Read Matthew 20:1–16.

Does God promise to bless us equally, or does God promise to supply our needs?

> ...God will meet all your needs according to his glorious riches in Christ Jesus.
>
> *Philippians* 4:19

Is it hard to love those who seem more richly blessed? Is there something Christians can do to make it easier?

Just Passing Through(10 *minutes)*

On your deathbed what do you imagine you would covet? Why? Is this perspective the most logical and useful in light of eternity?

What God Covets(10 *minutes)*

According to scripture, whose possession are we at birth?

> ...The whole world is under the control of the evil one.
>
> 1 *John* 5:19

What is God's response?

> For (the Lord) has rescued us from the dominion of darkness and brought us into the Kingdom of the Son He loves.
>
> *Colossians* 1:13

Does God covet us because of our goodness or because of His?

Wrap Up (5 minutes)

Share your prayer requests with one another.

Confirm the date and location of the next meeting.

Close by reading out loud the following prayer.

Dear God,

Lead us to simplicity. Lead us to what truly satisfies. Lead us away from the curse of comparison to the place where we are content with You and Your provision. Lord, this life is not fair, but to be free of envy, it doesn't have to be. Help us to rest in Your presence, confident that You will satisfy our deepest desires according to Your riches in glory. Amen.

Postlude:
A Benefit of Obedience

Immediately after World War II, Nazi leaders were put on trial for crimes against humanity. These were the infamous Nuremberg Trials. The evidence was overwhelming that the defendants had served to exterminate six million Jews! Even so, most defended themselves with the explanation they were simply obeying orders.

As a response to this trial and the questions it raised about the psychology of following orders, Dr. Stanley Milgram, a psychologist at Yale University, decided to construct his now famous experiment on obedience and its relation to authority. Dr. Milgrim invited volunteers from the community to participate in the experiment. One at a time, each volunteer was seated at a desk with an electrical meter atop it. They were told their meter controlled electrical current attached to a person who sat unseen behind a screen. They were also told the experiment was all about the effects of punishment on the learning process. The person behind the screen would be asked a series of questions, and each time they answered incorrectly the volunteers were to administer a shock of ever-increasing voltage from the meter at their desk.

What the volunteers were not told, however, was that the person behind the screen was actually an actor and that the real experiment was to measure just how far the volunteers would go to obey orders and punish the person behind the screen with electrical shock when told to do so. What Dr. Milgram's experiment discovered was—excuse the pun—shocking. Even with the actor behind the screen moaning in pain and shouting that they had a heart condition, still 60 percent of the volunteers would obey their instructors to increase the voltage all the way up to 450 volts—which was clearly marked on the meter as "deadly" voltage!

Dr. Milgrim's conclusion was "If a system of death camps were set up in the United States of the sort we had seen in Nazi Germany, one would be able to find sufficient personnel for those camps in any medium-sized American town."

I share this to ask a simple question. Why are so many so willing to obey human authority yet stubbornly refuse to obey God?

We go to great lengths to obey others—especially those in authority. We wear clothes that look silly on us all because fashion authorities like Versace tell us to. We buy technology we don't need and can't afford all because someone like Bill Gates tells us to. We compromise our morals and surrender our integrity because celebrities like Madonna tell us to. Yet when God tries to tell us something we dig in our heels and refuse to obey. Why?

Webster's dictionary employs the word "submit" to define obedience— "to *submit* to the …command of authority." In other words, to obey God would be to submit to Him. But the overwhelming evidence is that most of us just don't submit to God. We may embrace the belief that God exists, and that He loves, forgives, and blesses. We may trust that God has a plan and a purpose for our life, and that He won't fail and forsake us. We may even believe that Jesus rose from the grave, and that eternal life is ours by virtue of God's own sacrifice on our behalf. We may *believe,* but when it comes to actually acting in obedience to our beliefs, most of us simply refuse. Our stiff-necked and hardheaded nature simply finds it impossible to reliably obey God. There are a multitude of explanations for this, but the most obvious is that we just don't believe there is enough of a benefit. We simply refuse to submit to the Lord because deep down we're convinced that obedience to God is a dry hole and an empty promise.

"What's in It for Me?"

In today's egocentric, me-first-world, one question must first be answered first before all others. The question is this, "What's in it for me?" Of course, when it comes to obedience, we all know that the answer is easy. Obedience is a key attribute to any long-term success and satisfaction. After all, you won't climb high in your career if you have trouble obeying superiors? You risk your health if you refuse to obey your doctor? Marital bliss will elude you if you refuse to obey your wife or husband? Obedience is key to much of what is good in life. Obedience is a first principle parents need to instill in their children, and it's a first principle God must inspire in each of us to lead us out of the sins that hold us hostage.

When Moses was nearing his death, he summarized all that God had taught him with this observation about obedience.

> I have set before you ...life and good, death and evil. If you *obey* the commandments of the Lord ...then you shall live and multiply, and the Lord will bless you in the land ... But if your heart turns away, and you will not hear (obey) ...you shall perish...
>
> *Deuteronomy* 30:15–18 *(*RSV*)*

According to Moses obedience to God is a life or death matter! What's more, Scripture promises other benefits to those who obey. Let me cite chapter and verse:

Prosperity— "Obey ...His commandments ...that you may prosper in all that you do."

(1 Kings 2:3)

Blessing— "...blessings shall come upon you ...if you obey the voice of the Lord..."

(Deuteronomy 28:2)

Love— "If you obey ...you will remain in my love."

(John 15:10)

Salvation— "...eternal salvation for all who obey him."

(Hebrews 5:9)

God offers abundant blessings to anyone who chooses to *obey* Him. Here, let me highlight this relationship between blessing and obedience by using the illustration of how we handle our personal finances.

God promises that when we obey Him and give 10 percent of our income to His work (the tithe), He will open the doors of heaven and pour down on us an overflowing blessing.

> Bring the full tithes ...put me to the test, says the Lord of hosts, if I will not open the windows of heaven for you and pour down for you an overflowing blessing.
>
> *Malachi* 3:10

It is an extravagant promise! However we can read it, study it, translate the ancient Hebrew of it, and even tell other people all about it, yet the only way to find out if God is true to His word is to actually *obey* it. To just read about it or to listen to the preacher is not enough. You've got to do it yourself to find out whether God is true to His word. You've got to follow through and obey.

The spiritual principle here is simple: One step in obedience will teach you more about God than reading a hundred and one pages of Scripture! Indeed, we only know as much about God as our obedience reveals. Let me repeat this because it merits repetition. We only know as much about God as our obedience reveals! Personal experience with God comes through what happens after we obey Him!

Another example is praise. The Scripture says God wants us to praise Him… that "when the praises go up, the blessings come down." But some try to reverse the order of this principle… they want to offer praise only after having received the blessing. They want to praise the Lord only after God has secured their health and wealth. But obeying God means first to praise Him in all circumstances, the good and the bad alike; and when we do, He promises that the blessings will fall. The only way we can find out whether or not this promise is true is to put it into practice. Like I said, we learn infinitely more about God through one step of obedience than we do in a thousand and one prayers. God wants us to grow spiritually in an intimate relationship with Him, and the best way to do this is via the pathway of obedience.

Abraham and Sarah

Knowing God through obedience is well illustrated in the Bible's story of Abraham and Sarah.

Four thousand years ago, a man named Abram and his wife Sarai lived in Haran (now modern-day border of Turkey with Syria). But it came to pass that God spoke directly to Abram, saying,

> Go from your country and your kindred …to the land that I will show you …and I will bless you.
>
> *Genesis* 12:1–3

God spoke a promise to Abram after which Abram had to decide whether or not to obey. Keep in mind he didn't have the benefit of Scripture—the Bible hadn't yet been written. He didn't have the support of a synagogue, they didn't yet exist. Neither did Abram have a prophet to consult because they too hadn't yet come into practice. The only thing Abram had to confirm God's voice was the discernment of his own heart.

There are different ways Abram could have responded. He could have ignored God's voice—this would have been the *secular choice.* He could have talked it over with his wife—this would have been the *family values choice.* He could have written God's words down and memorized them—this would have been the *academic choice.* He could have formed a small study group or posted God's message on his refrigerator—this would have been the *self-improvement choice.* But instead, Abram chose simply to *obey.* He submitted himself to God's authority and did exactly what God told him to do—he left his home and family and traveled by faith to a new land. In doing so he learned more about God than you or I will ever learn from a book. For his obedience Abraham became known as the father of not one faith but three: Judaism, Christianity, and Islam!

The point of Abraham's story is simple: even though Abraham and Sarah didn't have the benefit of a Bible, a church, collective worship, ecclesiastic tradition, or any of the other spiritual tools we tend to take for granted today; nevertheless because they were willing to obey they grew to know God intimately. Abraham and Sarah knew as much about God as their obedience informed them.

At the risk of stating the obvious, Abraham and Sarah benefited from obeying God in two ways. First, and most practically, God led them to the Promised Land where they were blessed with wealth and a son! Second, and more profoundly, their obedience revealed to them who God was, and enabled both of them to establish a personal relationship with their Creator.

And what's in it for you should you choose to obey God's voice? What's a benefit of obedience? Well, if you want to know God—His purpose for your life, and His pleasure in your soul, if you want to climb spiritual mountaintops, if you want a supernatural visitation, if you want to feel God's presence and discern His movements in your life, if you want to be led into the promised land that God has for you, then obedience is the way to go. Again, we experience only as much about God as our obedience informs us.

Francis Bacon expressed obedience as the relationship between what we believe and what we do:

> It is not what men eat, but what they digest that makes them strong; not what we gain (earn), but what we save that makes us rich; not what we read, but what we remember that makes us learned; not what we preach or pray, but what we believe and practice that makes us Christian.

The crucial question is always— "Will you obey God? Will you do what He tells you?" Your answer will determine just how intimately you know and enjoy God. It's one thing to say that you believe in God, but it's quite another to obey Him. Belief requires no action, but obedience does.

Here you are wise to keep in mind that you get no extra credit with God for obedience.

It is common to think that God owes you something when you obey—like a well-trained dog who expects a treat for following orders. This, by the way, is the real religion of many Americans—obeying God just enough to put God in their debt, so that when they pray they have enough credits to get what they want. But obedience leverages nothing with God. Using obedience to control and manipulate God gets us nowhere.

In most church buildings, you will find carved somewhere in stone or wood the prayer of Jesus that says, "Thy will be done." This is the prayer of perfect obedience. It is what is said when we are finally willing to trust God enough to obey on His terms. It is when we surrender our own personal agenda and embrace obeying His. And as I've said, in submitting ourselves to God's authority, we come to know Him personally—not as we want God to be, or as we imagine Him to be, or as we presume He should be—but as He really is. We finally enter into a personal and profound relationship with the living God.

And What if We Fail?

But what if we fail in our attempt to obey? Here we enter into the beautiful paradox of the Christian gospel, for whether we succeed or fail in our attempt to obey, we win both ways. Let me explain.

When we successfully obey, we learn about God's character. We learn that God is faithful to His promises, good to His word, and that He will neither fail nor forsake us. God's character is absolutely reliable. He always comes through. We can be 100 percent confident in building our lives upon the spiritual principle of obedience to Him and His word.

But when our obedience fails, we have occasion to experience something else about God. In failure we learn about the heart of God ...that God is compassionate and merciful, and that "he takes care of those who turn to Him" (Nahum 1:7). When we fail in our effort to obey, we will experience for ourselves God's persistent presence—that our failures do not cause Him to flee offended and outraged. Indeed, in our failure we discover that God draws that much closer to us knowing that we need Him more in our failure than we do in our success.

This is the incredible win-win quality of the Christian gospel. When we obey, we learn the character of God; and when we fail in our obedience, we learn the heart of God. Both are glorious and wonderful. Both can transport us from the dinginess of everyday life to the very throne room of heaven. And both inform us of just who God is—faithful and compassionate, slow to anger and full of steadfast love. Like I said, it's in obedience, whether successful or unsuccessful, that we learn just who God is. For we learn only as much about God as our obedience reveals! Not a bad benefit for anyone who sincerely desires to know God in all His splendor, glory, and surprise.

Stanley Milgrim's famous experiment on obedience in its relationship to authority demonstrated just how low we can all sink in following orders. But the Scriptures also proclaim just how high we can all rise if we humble ourselves, welcome Jesus Christ as the Lord and master of our lives, and *obey* Him! Amen.

Study Guide: the Benefit of Obedience!

90 Minutes

Introduction (15 minutes)

Briefly

Have each participant share what has been the biggest benefit studying the Ten Commandments! Each may describe one specific change they will make as a result of their participation.

Opening Discussion/Warm Up (10 minutes)

Why do you suppose so many are so willing to obey people, and yet are reluctant to obey God?

What's in It for Me?(30 minutes)

Read aloud the following paragraph:

> Obedience is a key attribute to any long-term success and satisfaction. After all, you won't climb high in your career if you have trouble obeying superiors? You risk your health if you refuse to obey your doctor? Marital bliss will elude you if you refuse to obey your wife or husband? Obedience is key to much of what is good in life. Obedience is a first principle parents need to instill in their children, and it's a first principle God must inspire in each of us to lead us out of the sins that hold us hostage.

Review some of the biblical blessings for obeying God.

> *Prosperity*— "Obey …His commandments …that you may prosper in all that you do."
>
> (*1 Kings 2:3*)

Blessing— "...blessings shall come upon you ...if you obey the voice of the Lord..."

Love— "If you obey ...you will remain in my love."
(John 15:10*)*

Salvation— "...eternal salvation for all who obey him."
(Hebrews 5:9*)*

There are many blessings (both secular and spiritual) connected to obedience, *but* how do we know that the promise of these blessings are real?

Discuss the following statement:

> One step in obedience will teach you more about God than reading a hundred and one pages of scripture! Indeed, we only know as much about God as our obedience reveals.

Share stories of things you learned about God because of your obedience.

*Abraham and Sarah(*10 *minutes)*

Four thousand years ago, God directed Abraham and Sarah to leave their home and family and travel to a new land. What were their choices for a response?

Did Abraham and Sarah learn anything about God through their obedience to Him?

When you sense God directing you to do something, what are your choices for a response? Is it any easier or harder to obey today than it was four thousand years ago?

Are we likely to learn the same sort of things about God via our obedience as Abraham and Sarah did in theirs?

Read the following quote from Francis Bacon:

> It is not what men eat, but what they digest that makes them strong; not what we gain (earn), but what we save that makes us rich; not what we read, but what we remember that makes us learned; not what we preach or pray, but what we believe and practice that makes us Christian.

No Extra Credit(5 minutes)

Does God owe you anything when you obey?

What if We Fail?(15 minutes)

Is there any benefit in attempting to obey God and failing?

When do we learn the most about the heart of God—in our success or in our failures?

In the New Testament, when did Jesus's apostles learn the most about Him, in they succeed in their obedience or in their failure? Give an example.

Discuss the following statement:

> When we obey we learn the character of God, and when we fail in our obedience we learn the heart of God.

Wrap Up (5 minutes)

Share your prayer requests with one another.

Confirm the date and location of the next meeting.

Close by reading out loud the following prayer.

Dear God,

Help us to put our trust in *You,* and obey. Amen.

Endnotes

1 Micklethwait, John and Wooldridge, Adrian. God Is Back. Penguin Books, NYC, 2009, p. 16

2 Micklethwait & Wooldridge, God Is Back. Penguin Books, NYC, 2009, p.13

3 Vowell, Sarah. *The Wordy Shipmates.* Riverhead Books, NYC, 2008, p. 77

4 Seamands, David A., *God's Blueprint for Living,* Bristol Books, Wilmore, KY. 1988, p. 116–7

5 Seamands, David A., *God's Blueprint for Living,* Bristol Books, Wilmore, KY. 1988, p. 116–7

6 http://www.barna.org/FlexPage.aspx?Page=BarnaUpdateNarrow&BarnaUpdateID=194

7 USA Today July 1st 2006 Joe Saltzman, http://www.accessmylibrary.com/coms2/summary_0286-23811519_ITM

8 http://www.allenaustinsearch.com/ssi_report.pdf

9 www.esermons.com/theResultsPage.asp?user_id=33487

10 Chittister, Joan. *The Ten Commandments, Laws of the Heart.* Orbis Books, Maryknoll, NY 2006 p. 121–2

Bibliography

Briscoe, Stuart. *The Ten Commandments, Playing by the Rules.* Wheaton: Herald Shaw Publishers, 1986.

Chittister, Joan. *The Ten Commandments, Laws of the Heart.* Maryknoll, NY: Orbis Books, 2006.

Davidman, Joy. Smoke on the Mountain, An Interpretation of the Ten Commandments. Philadelphia: The Westminster Press, 1953.

Calvin, John. *Sermons on the Ten Commandments.* Eugene, OR: Wipf & Stock Publishers, 2000.

Federer, William J. *The Ten Commandments and Their Influence on American Law.* St. Louis, MO: Amerisearch, Inc., 2003.

Hedges, Chris. Losing Moses on the Freeway, the Ten Commandments in America. New York: Free Press, 2005.

Holbert, John C. *The Ten Commandments.* Nashville: Abingdon Press, 2002.

Lehmann, Paul L. *The Decalogue and a Human Future.* Eugene, OR: Wipf & Stock Publishers, 1995.

Luther, Martin. The Large Catechism. Philadelphia: Fortress Press, 1959.

Micklethwait, John and Wooldridge, Adrian. God Is Back. New York: Penguin Books, 2009

Peck, M. Scott. *The Road Less Traveled.* New York: Simon & Schuster Inc., 1978.

Peck, M. Scott. *The People of the Lie.* New York: Simon & Schuster Inc., 1983.

Seamands, David A. *God's Blueprint for Living.* Wilmore, KY: Bristol Books, 1988.

Vines, Jerry. *Basic Bible Sermons on the Ten Commandments.* Nashville: Broadman Press, 1992.

Vowell, Sarah. *The Wordy Shipmates.* New York: Riverhead Books, 2008.

Eight Translation New Testament, Wheaton, IL: Tyndale House Publisher, Inc., 1974.

The New Oxford Annotated Bible, New Revised Standard Version. Bruce Metzger & Roland Murphy. New York: Oxford University Press. 1991.

Holy Bible, King James Version. C.I.Scofield, New York: Oxford University Press. 1967.

The Word in Life Study Bible, New King James Version, Nashville: Thomas Nelson Publishers. 1993.

Good News Bible, Today's English Version. New York: American Bible Society. 1992.

The Message, The Bible in Contemporary Language, Eugene H. Peterson, Colorado Springs, CO: NavPress, 2002.

The Living Bible, Kenneth N. Taylor, Wheaton, Illinois: Tyndale House Publishers, 1971.